George Washington Carver

THE STORY OF A GREAT AMERICAN

GEORGE WASHINGTON CARVER

The Story of a Great American

by ANNE TERRY WHITE

Illustrated by DOUGLAS GORSLINE

RANDOM HOUSE · NEW YORK

The author wishes to express her thanks to Doubleday & Company for the use of 600 words from GEORGE WASHINGTON CARVER by Rackham Holt, copyright 1943 by Doubleday & Company, Inc.

SECOND PRINTING

Published in New York by Random House, Inc.
and simultaneously in Toronto, Canada by
Random House of Canada, Ltd.

Library of Congress Catalog Card Number: 53–6262

Manufactured in the U.S.A.

For Deborah Ann

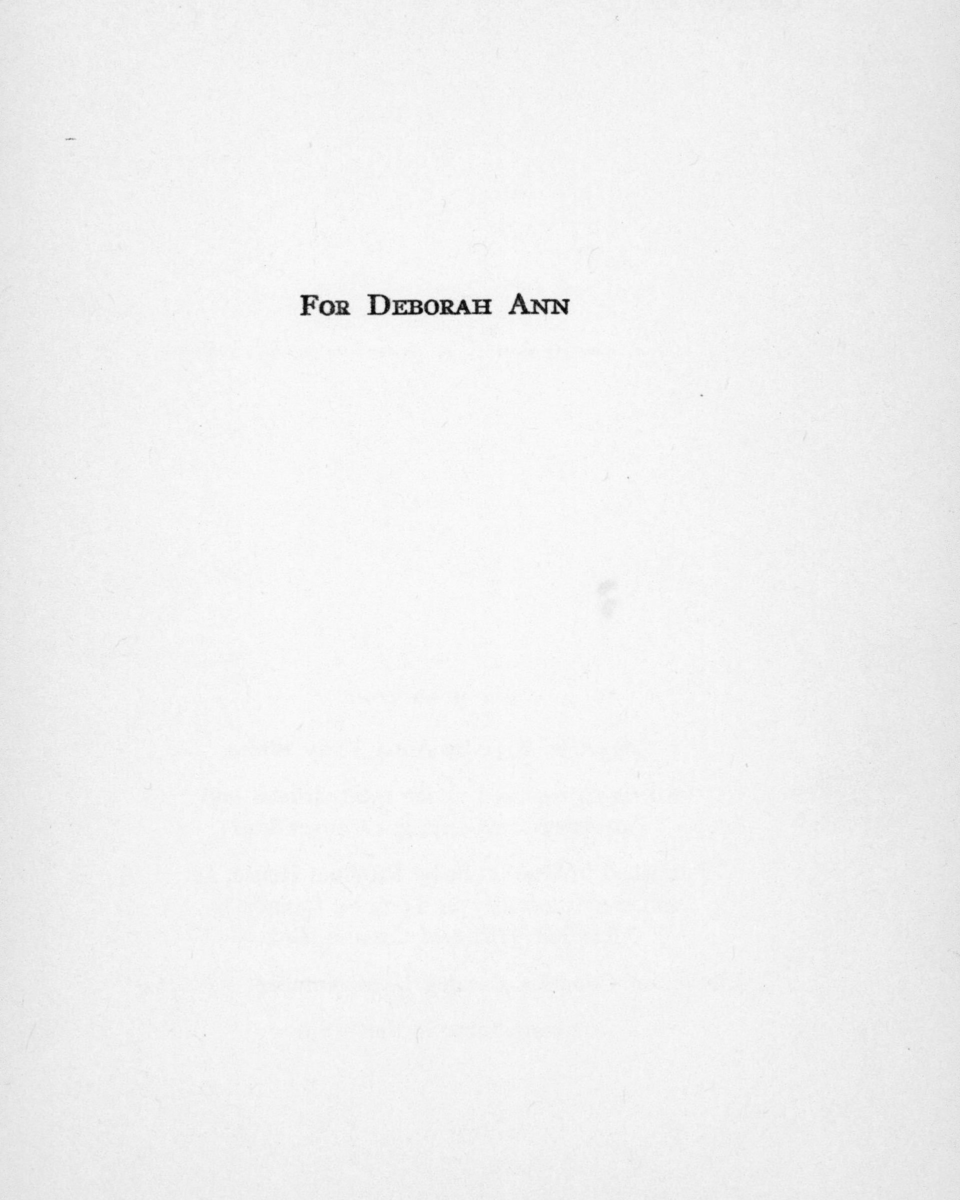

CONTENTS

George Washington Carver

THE STORY OF A GREAT AMERICAN

A Race Horse for a Baby

1

WINTERS ARE COLD IN THE FOOTHILLS OF THE OZARKS. In January of 1861 the ground was frozen a foot down. Day and night in Moses Carver's one-room farmhouse a great log was kept burning on the hearth.

Susan Carver sat strangely idle by it on a bitter night after the hard day's work was done. Though a half finished sock was in her lap, for once her fingers were still. In the far corner of the room Moses Carver lay abed. The farm wife glanced now and then at her husband's pale face, lit up by a tallow dip, but neither of them spoke. For both were thinking anxious thoughts.

Suddenly the crunch of footsteps outside and a loud knocking sent the woman hurrying to open up.

"Who is it, Sue?"

The farmer raised himself painfully on his elbow and peered around the post of the wide wooden bed. By the open door his wife stood holding the candle high. She was talking to someone, but who it was he couldn't make out. The howling January wind that sent the smoke billowing from the fireplace nearly blew the flame out and drowned the voices.

The door slammed. Susan Carver clattered across the rough wooden floor to the bed.

"It's that bushwhacker you sent to steal our Mary back," she said in a choked voice as she set the candle down.

"Has he got her?" Moses Carver demanded.

"No! Just the baby," his wife answered. "He's got it out there tied to his saddle. How the poor. . . ."

She broke off as again the crunch of footsteps sounded on the frozen ground. Running to the door, she flung it open. Again smoke from the fireplace swirled into the room. Through the haze Moses Carver could see his wife take a bundle over to the other bed, where little Jim was sleeping.

"Well, Bentley?" the farmer called out impatiently.

The visitor had taken off his visored cap and stood twirling it in his hands. His long, unkempt hair fell about his face.

"Ain't seen no trace of your slave girl, Carver," he said in a low, harsh voice. "I been fifty mile down into Arkansas. Couldn't come up with them raiders."

"But you said. . . ."

"Take it any way you like, Carver," Bentley broke in. "I ain't found her. Some told me she's been sent down river. One said he'd seen her go north with soldiers. Most folks thinks as she's dead."

"Seems like if you found her baby. . . ." Carver began again and stopped.

Bentley shrugged his shoulders. "The raiders must've got tired bothering with it and left it behind," he said. "A couple of women had it."

Over on the other bed Susan Carver had been struggling meantime to undo the man's rough coat in which the baby was bundled. A smothered coughing came from inside.

"Reckon it's alive yet," Bentley said and walked over.

A cry escaped the honest farm wife as the puny black baby came to view. It lay there choking, gasping for breath. Its matchstick arms beat the air weakly.

"Awful small," Bentley commented. "All head. How old do you reckon it is?"

"A year—just," Susan Carver answered promptly. "He was born 1860, year ago this month."

She had wrapped the baby warm in her shawl and now held the little creature upright against herself. "There, there, George," she crooned to comfort it. "There, baby, there."

The men looked on in silence.

"It's whooping cough," Susan Carver explained. "Remember, Mose? I mixed honey with tansy for him the day they carried Mary off. The cup's down there in her cabin yet."

Bentley jerked his thumb toward the handsome three-year-old Negro child asleep in the second bed. "I see you got the older boy in here with you," he remarked.

"Yes, we've got Jim safe in here with us," Susan Carver repeated.

Her free hand drew the covers close about the sleeping boy. Then, lowering her voice, she said, "If I live to be a hundred, I'll not forget that night. Soon as we heard the raiders, my man made for the cabin. 'Run, Mary!' he says. Then he snatches the boy out of his trundle bed, and off to the woods. But Mary!

Before she could no more than scream, they had her and the baby on a horse."

Bentley shook his head. "These is bad times," he said. "I seen a lot of things in this here State of Missouri, bushwhacking, fighting them Kansas raiders. Pretty near had my bellyful. Guess you've had yours, too, Carver," he added with a grin. "Ain't many took what you took."

Everybody in Diamond Grove and even up to Neosho, eight miles away, knew the raiders hadn't been satisfied to steal Moses Carver's slave girl. Either they, or others like them, had come again a few days later to get the thrifty German's money. All the German immigrants from Illinois were doing well. But Moses Carver was especially marked out for plunder. A man who bred race horses was sure to have silver stowed away.

"Where's your money? Tell us where you got it hid!" the raiders had demanded.

Moses Carver hadn't opened his mouth. They had strung him up by his thumbs to his own walnut tree that grew by the house. They'd taken burning coals from the fireplace and put them to his feet. But even then the sturdy farmer hadn't revealed where his money was hid.

"It won't be long before I'm up and about again," he said to Bentley. "My wife's been putting plantain leaves to my feet—don't hurt as much any more." Then in a different tone he added, "Well, Bentley, what you want to take for George? I haven't as much as people think, but I mean to pay you well for Mary's baby. My wife's done nothing but cry since we lost the girl."

The bushwhacker stopped twirling his cap. He stood shifting his weight from foot to foot while he considered the question.

"I ain't brought back your girl," he said after a moment, "so I can't take that forty acre of timberland you promised me. But if you say it's fair, Carver, I'll take that race horse you said you'd give me over and above. I'll take the race horse for my trouble, Carver."

"It's fair," Moses Carver declared. "Take the race horse and welcome. . . . But I want you to know," he added, "you're getting $300 for the baby—that's what Pacer's worth. Sue, you set George down here by me. My wife will show you, Bentley, where we've got the horse hid."

Susan Carver threw her husband's coat about her shoulders. "You have to go a ways into the woods," she said.

The wild winter wind almost tore the door from her hand. The fire smoked and billowed, then shot roaring up into the chimney. Shadows danced on the walls of the bare, one-room house.

Pioneer Farm

2

MOSES CARVER DIDN'T BEGRUDGE THE $300 RACE HORSE the baby had cost him; for George was Mary's child, and Mary had been almost a member of the family. But there was another and stronger reason. The farmer's conscience bothered him.

Here he was, a man who didn't believe in slavery, and what had he done? He had himself owned a human being as one owns a horse or ox. To be sure, in the thirty odd years he had lived in Missouri he had bought just the one slave. But one was as bad as a hundred—wasn't the principle the same?

Moses Carver had tried hard to still his conscience at the time. Hewing a home out of the wilderness was killing work, he told himself. For five and twenty years he and Sue had toiled and toiled, doing alone everything that had to be done on the 140-acre farm. But finally Sue was no longer able to keep up with the work. What with the spinning and weaving and curing and churning and the thousand other endless tasks, she was getting worn out. And there was no servant to be hired.

So Moses had weakened. "The girl will be better off with us than with another," he had said to Susan that time six years ago. And he had gone to his neighbor, Colonel Grant.

Moses had gone, still fighting with himself. He had put down $700 and he had returned with thirteen-year-old Mary. In his pocket was a paper that warranted the girl to be "sound in body and mind and a slave for life."

Sound in body and mind. Certainly Mary had been that. She had been bright and quick and clever with her hands—and gay, too. She had gone singing about her work—that is, till just lately. That was when word came from the Grant place that the father of her children had been killed. "Hauling wood," they said, "a heavy log. . . ."

No. Pacer was not too much to give for Mary's baby. Peace of mind was worth $300. Mary's boy would have a chance to grow into a decent man.

But there were times when Sue and Moses wondered whether George would grow up at all. He was so thin, so delicate, always down with croup or one thing and another. When he could walk once across the room without falling, it was a victory. Talk? It seemed he'd never learn to talk. And after he did, he stammered so that half the time you couldn't make out what he was saying in that high, piping, birdlike voice of his.

Altogether he looked like a baby bird, all head and mouth. Beside the sturdy, handsome Jim, George with his spindly arms and legs felt decidedly at a disadvantage. He couldn't do any of the hard outside work that made Jim feel so important. George couldn't lift, couldn't push, couldn't drag.

Jim followed Uncle Mose around and helped in all the things the farmer was doing. George stayed close to Aunt Sue. One thing only consoled him for that comical body of his—his wonderfully long, slim fingers. His fingers seemed to have magic in them. They could do anything George wanted them to.

The boy saw Aunt Sue knitting. "Why can't I do that with my hands?" he thought. Coming close, he watched how she moved her fingers. There were turkey feathers out in the yard. George ran out and stripped some, leaving just a little tuft at the end—and there were needles for him. He unraveled the top of an old stocking and a mitten—and there was wool for him. He learned to knit.

He saw Aunt Sue crocheting. "Why can't I do that with my hands?" he said. He borrowed her hook and made patterns of his own, patterns of ferns and flowers and birds.

He was always at Aunt Sue's elbow when he was in the house, always learning to do things with his hands. He learned bits of cooking. Until they got the parlor cook stove years later, all the cooking had to be done in the fireplace. George learned to mix the corn batter. He'd pour it in the skillet, fit on a tight lid, and set it on the coals. Then he would pile more coals on the lid. And soon the savory smell of fatty corn bread would fill the room.

There was plenty of work on the Carver farm—more work than all of them could do—and, sick or well, George did his share. On their 140 acres Uncle Mose and Aunt Sue "lived at home"—they grew and made practically everything they used. Only coffee and sugar came from outside. And even these they got by exchanging produce for them.

Four o'clock in the morning summer and winter everybody was up. The horses had to be tended, the cows milked, the poultry fed. There were sheep to shear, and wool and flax to spin, and cloth to weave, and deer skins to tan, and shoes to make. There were trees to cut down, and wood to saw and split and stack and carry in.

Corn and flax and hemp had to be planted and cared for. Vegetables needed to be weeded and picked and stored. Apples and peaches and pears and blackberries had to be dried in the sun. From the woods hazelnuts and pecans and walnuts and butternuts must be brought in. There were the eggs to find and the butter to churn and the cheese to make and the beehives to care for. There was bacon and ham and venison to cure, lard and soap to make.

Was someone in the family sick? Did a horse have the botts? Run, George, cut bark from the north side of the tree. Dig roots, gather herbs.

Was there cloth to be dyed? Get oak bark for black, hickory for yellow, chestnut for brown.

Yes, there was plenty of work for all. But there was good living for all, too. Only once did George remember a time when there wasn't enough to eat. Or perhaps he didn't remember at all but only remembered their telling him about it.

The Civil War was still raging then, and lawless bands roamed Missouri. Again raiders came to Moses Carver's farm. This time they tipped over his beehives one by one and found his money hidden under one.

But the farmer's spirit hadn't been broken. He had worked all the harder after that—and the hungry times had passed. Again there was plenty for all.

That's how George always remembered his years with Aunt Sue and Uncle Mose—plenty for all, everything used, nothing wasted.

The Plant Doctor

3

"I DON'T KNOW WHAT'S THE MATTER WITH THAT FERN, George. It used to fill this whole corner."

Mrs. Baynham threw the last drops of her dish-water into the garden and wiped her hands on her apron. She sighed. Colonel Grant's place, which she had bought a few years back, was too much for her. Before the War, big gardens like this were all right —you had slaves to care for them. But now the War was over, the slaves were free, and you had to tend your garden yourself. Colonel Grant hadn't been able to handle it, and neither could she.

George crouched down to look. A few green fronds still stood upright in the center of the fern, but all the outer leaves were brown and dry. A great circle of brown lay on the ground.

The boy passed his fingers gently over a stalk, then felt the earth about the plant. He thought a moment, then said confidently, "I c-c-can make your f-f-fern well for you. L-l-let me take it away."

"Will you be sure to bring it back?"

"I'll bring it back."

George got a piece of sacking. He dug the plant up, set it on the sacking, and tied the ends tight.

"I'll b-b-bring it back in the fall," he said.

He loved to help plants grow. Perhaps it was because George was so often sick himself that sick plants spoke to him. He would nurse a dying plant as Aunt Sue nursed him when he was down—with the same watchfulness, with the same tenderness. He had a secret plot in the woods. He would take the sick plants there and doctor them. This one needed shade. That one needed new soil.

The neighbors called him the Plant Doctor. They had learned that, small as he was, the little black boy knew what to do for sick plants.

"George, what's happening to my roses? The leaves are getting yellow and spotted."

"You have to give them s-s-sun, Mrs. Selby. Roses want sun," he would say.

"George, something's killing my lilies."

George would dig around and bring up grubs. "That's what's doing it, Mrs. Swan."

If a plant was too far gone, he would dig it up and carry it to his forest greenhouse. He would bring water from the stream below his mother's cabin. Then he would shake the soil from the roots and bury them in fresh earth. He never lost a plant.

The women talked to Aunt Sue about him. "How did your George get to know so much about plants? He's a regular little Plant Doctor," they said.

Aunt Sue was pleased to hear nice things about her George.

"Land only knows," she answered. "That boy has been asking questions about growing things since he could ask anything at all. It's always been 'Why, why?' with him."

Yes, always it had been that way. And before he learned to speak, it had been that way. George had wondered and silently asked why.

Why are sunflowers yellow and wild roses pink? Why is some rose moss part one color, part another, some striped, some spotted? If I plant a pink flower by a yellow one, will the colors mix? Why do morning glories close so early? Why do leaves on one and the same sassafras have different shapes? Why do gourds grow on vines and pears on trees?

He wanted to know the name of everything that grew. If no one could tell him, he made up a name himself. He felt he did not know a plant unless he could call it by name.

As soon as the weather permitted, George spent his Sundays in the woods. Uncle Mose and Aunt Sue didn't go to church; so the boy had the whole day to do with as he pleased. Often he left before it was light. At four o'clock in the morning the woods had things to say to him.

What did he do there in the woods alone?

George watched the wild creatures stirring, he listened to the early din the birds made. He lifted the dead, brown leaves to see the jack-in-the-pulpits coming up. He raised up bits of dead bark and watched the insects crawl. He broke off bits of fungus from a rotting stump.

Sometimes he just sat on a tree root and listened to the rustling of the leaves. There was something in the woods that carried George out of and beyond himself. There was a spirit there—something big, something he couldn't touch or name, something he could only feel. A voice seemed to say to him, "You are not alone, George. I am with you, you belong to me."

He never felt frightened in the woods—the woods were more his home than his house was. With a couple of corn dodgers in his pocket he could stay away the whole day. And at supper time he came home with pockets full of rocks and mica and acorns, feathers and leaves and grasses and a frog perhaps. Aunt Sue called it all "trash" and wouldn't let him take his "foolishness" into the house.

Yes, Jim may have been the one that chopped wood. But the woods belonged to George.

To make things and to make things grow—these were the weekday occupations that kept George happy. But the Sunday spirit of the woods never quite left him. It was as though George carried a wonderful secret about with him, a secret about a very special friend who loved and understood and watched over him.

One day George had a dream. He dreamed that out in a corn field he saw a watermelon lying. The watermelon had been cut open and partly eaten. The rind was lying on the ground. He could see just where it lay against a corn hill out of which three stalks were growing.

But that was not the important part of the dream. The important part was that right beside the watermelon rind a knife was lying. It was a lady's knife, not much broader than a pencil. It had a black handle and two blades.

Now of all things the one George wanted most was a knife. Though he could always borrow one of Uncle Mose's hunting knives, that wasn't at all the same thing as having a knife of your own. So he clung to his dream. Uncle Mose had often told him that a hungry chicken dreamed of grain. But George didn't want to believe that you dreamed about the things you were hungry for. He thought the dream was a special message to him.

As soon as he could get away from the breakfast table, he made off over the fences. The corn field of his dream wasn't one of their own. He knew exactly which one of their neighbors the dream corn field belonged to, and even while he ran he knew he was going to the very spot. Sure enough, there were the three cornstalks and the half-eaten watermelon and the rinds. And there was the knife!

What would Uncle Mose say to that? Wasn't this proof positive that someone was watching over him?

Out into the Wide World

4

NOW THAT GEORGE HAD A KNIFE OF HIS OWN, THERE were more things his hands could do. He made himself a cornstalk fiddle. With some hair from a horse's tail, he strung a bow. And he made music.

All the little white boys and girls with whom he played came around to hear him make music. None of them could play a cornstalk fiddle the way he could.

Then in a wonderful sort of adventure George discovered painting.

He was up at the Baynham place one day where, ever since the healing of the fern, he was a welcome visitor. Mrs. Baynham had taken him into the kitchen for a treat. Somehow he had been left alone, and for once he got up enough courage to try and see what the rest of the big, brick and frame house looked like. His mother and father had both been slaves on the old Grant place, and George was very curious about it.

He stole out into the hall, opened a big white door, and found himself in the parlor. There was a rug on the floor. Big, soft-looking chairs covered with cloth stood on it. Then George looked up at the walls and for a minute his heart stopped beating. A whole row of people was staring down at him. He wanted to run but was frozen to the spot. Then he realized that the people weren't real. He had never seen portraits before.

So here was something else people did with their hands. Well, if others could do it, he could, too.

George didn't have any paper or pencils or brushes or paints. So he scratched his pictures on rocks and glass and old cans and buckets. Out of berries and roots and bark he made himself colors. And he painted. It was a secret—he wouldn't have dared to bring such "foolishness" into the house.

His mind was as hungry as his hands. Aunt Sue, who saw it, gave George an old blue-back spelling book. It started out with the alphabet and meaningless sounds like *ba, ca, da,* then went on to real words. George learned the alphabet. He learned the sounds. Then he learned to read and spell every word in the book.

One evening at the supper table the boy came out with something he had been carrying around in his mind for a long time.

"Uncle Mose, I want to go to school."

Uncle Mose frowned into his pea soup and buttered another piece of corn bread before he answered. The question of the children's education troubled him.

"How are you going to do it, boy?" he asked gently. "You're colored. The school here won't take you. It's just for white children."

George knew that. He had already tried. But he was prepared for Uncle Mose's argument.

"There's a school for colored children in Neosho," he said.

Aunt Sue put down her spoon. "Neosho is eight

miles away, George," she said. "How would you go back and forth?"

"I wouldn't. I'd stay in Neosho," George explained.

"How would you live?" Jim put in. "Where would you stay?"

"I'll find me a place," George said confidently. "I'll help some lady do her work."

Uncle Mose looked questioningly across the table at Aunt Sue.

"Let him try, Mose," she said. "I know he's only ten and small for his age. But he's smart with his hands—you know that. And if he can't make out, he can always come home."

So it was settled. By the next afternoon Aunt Sue had his clothes clean.

"You wear your Sunday suit," she said as she helped George tie his things in a bandanna. "But put your shoes in your bundle. It would be a pity to wear them out on the road."

She stood waving to the boy as long as she could see him. With his bundle on a stick over his shoulder, how small he looked against the sky and the fields and the road! There he was—ten and going out into the wide world.

Aunt Sue sighed. For some reason she recalled how

George had coughed that night when the bushwhacker brought him home and how the man had said, "Reckon he's alive yet." The child was sick so much of the time still. How would he make out?

In George's mind there was no doubt. Ever since he had found his dream knife in the corn field, he had been more sure of himself. And, besides, Neosho wasn't altogether a strange place to him. Once every year Uncle Mose let him go there by himself to have a day's fun. On his last visit George had found out where the school for Negro children was. He had gone there and peeked in through the window and had seen a whole roomful of colored children sitting over their books. He knew just how to get there.

It was late afternoon when he got to Neosho. Up to this time George hadn't thought much beyond the school, but now he realized he had to find some place to sleep. He walked over the town and walked over it, every now and again coming back to the tumble-down one-room cabin that was the Lincoln School. His feet lagged more and more. Finally they gave out altogether.

But just then George saw a barn with its door wide open. From the darkness inside came the sweet smell of hay. George stepped in. Except for a horse that stood switching its tail in a stall, the place was empty.

George found the slats leading to the hayloft, buried himself in the hay, and went to sleep.

Early next morning he crept out—it wouldn't do to let anyone find him there. He was very hungry, having eaten nothing since noonday dinner the day before. What should he do about breakfast? He was sitting on a woodpile trying to solve that problem when a woman came out of a neat little house and walked straight towards him. She was small and had a light brown skin.

"Well, boy, you sure looks hungry," she said to George. Her eyes were like brown shoe buttons and danced when she spoke. "Help me bring in some sticks, and we'll have us some breakfast."

In the flash of an eye she had the fire going, and bacon frying, and coffee and corn bread on. All the time she bustled about, she chattered.

"Come all the way from Diamond to go to school! Now that's a right smart thing to do. Learning. That's what us colored folks needs. Ain't it lucky I came out just when you was sitting on the woodpile? School's right over the fence there. You couldn't be closer, George."

She set cups and plates on the bare wood table. "You got to have two names for school, though," she went on. "Carver's George? No, boy," she laughed.

"You got to make that George Carver. Now, our name's Watkins. You call me Aunt Mariah. All my children call me Aunt Mariah. And him," she said, pointing to a short, stubby man who had walked in from the next room, "that's my husband—you call him Uncle Andy."

Uncle Andy nodded pleasantly to George and sat down at the table. He seemed to take George as a matter of course.

"George Carver's going to stay with us a spell, Andy," Aunt Mariah said briefly. With that, she took the corn bread from the oven, cut it like a pie, and poured the coffee.

She had spoken about her children; so George was surprised to find no one besides Andy coming to the table. But as Aunt Mariah chattered on, the boy understood the reason. The children she spoke of and called hers were other women's children whom she had helped bring into the world. She and Andy, he learned, had no children of their own.

When breakfast was over, Mariah Watkins dipped hot water from a big iron pot that stood on the back of the stove. "Come on now, George," she said. "You got to be clean for school."

George didn't protest. Aunt Mariah scrubbed him and polished him and brushed him. Then she put a big apron around him and let him help till school time. With a full heart George washed the dishes and swept the floor and took scraps out to the chickens.

"You run along now and just you come right back here for your dinner," she said when they heard the school bell.

With her warm words ringing in his ears and her dancing eyes following him all the way, George climbed over the fence to begin his education.

His Own People

SCHOOL! THE WORD SENT A LITTLE SHIVER OF EXCITEMENT down George's spine.

As he gave his name to the young Negro lad who was the teacher, the boy's heart pounded. He unknotted his handkerchief and counted out pennies to pay for the book and the slate Mr. Frost gave him. Then, holding his treasures close against his chest, George pushed his way through the throng of children. Long, high benches filled all the floor space. He squeezed himself onto the end of one and opened his book.

George had never been among colored children before. As a matter of fact, until this morning he had never known any colored people at all except his brother Jim. Now as George sat leafing through his reading book and trying out his slate, he threw curious glances at his companions. Seventy-five children of every shade from yellow to dark brown squirmed and twisted and jostled one another on the hard, backless benches. The children had to fight for work space in the fourteen by sixteen foot cabin.

George fought for space, too. At first, with the buzzing and shuffling all around him, he found it hard to put his mind on his slate. But little by little he got used to the noise, the crowding, the heavy air. The magic of words and figures held him. He was surprised when it was noon. He took his reading book and slate over the fence to the Watkins house.

When he told Aunt Mariah how crowded the school was, her eyes stopped dancing. She stirred the fire hard and banged the stove lids in place.

"It's more crowded than you know, boy," she said in a voice George hadn't heard before. "It ain't only the children as is going to school—their fathers and their mothers is right there with them. Our people is hungry for learning, hungry."

And she told George how before the Civil War there was a law making it a crime for anyone to teach a slave to read or write. "Our people don't want their children to grow up in the dark like they did," she said.

While George washed his hands, Aunt Mariah set the table. All the time she kept on talking.

"There was a slave woman lived on our plantation," she said, "who could read fine. But she never let on she had learning. One day a no-good white girl told the mistress, 'Did you know your Lizzie can read?' The mistress sent for Lizzie right off. Course, Lizzie said, 'No. How come a slave woman like me should know reading?'

"Well, the mistress wouldn't believe her and wouldn't believe her. She kept setting traps for Lizzie. She'd leave out a newspaper to see if Lizzie would pick it up to read it. Or she'd say, 'What does it say on that bottle, Lizzie? I left my spectacles upstairs.' But Lizzie never let on. They couldn't catch her. And all the time she was teaching us in secret. That's how I come to know reading."

Aunt Mariah lifted the lid from a pot and stirred

the savory rice and peas. George snuffed the air hungrily. He couldn't wait to dig into the heaped up plate she set before him.

"George," Aunt Mariah said as she watched him enjoying his dinner, "just like you is hungry for that Hopping John, that's how our people is hungry for learning. You go and learn all you can, George. And then you be like Lizzie. Don't keep your learning just for yourself—give it all back to your people. And your people is going to bless you."

Aunt Mariah said she could read, but actually she could just barely pick out words here and there. She listened with wonder to anything George read to her. "I'm going to school right alongside of you, George," she would say.

In exchange there was a great deal she could teach George, and she set right out to do it.

"You've got your living to earn, you know, George," she said. "Now, you ain't big and strong. You can't get heavy laboring jobs like my Andy. You got to use them smart fingers of yours."

So she taught him how to cook. She taught him how to wash clothes and to starch and sprinkle and iron.

"You got to have your iron just right," she said.

She put her finger to her tongue, then touched the iron to test it. "And get it up into the corners like this."

George watched, fascinated, as the iron glided up and down and across the board, leaving behind smooth tucks and pleats and curly ruffles.

He would come home at noon, eat his dinner, then work over the washboard. Sometimes he would prop his book up in front of the washtub and scrub away till it was time to go back.

Stephen Frost didn't know a great deal himself, and it was not many months before he had taught George all he could. But George kept on going to school just the same, hoping to pick up a little more.

At the same time he put into practice what Aunt Mariah had taught him. Whenever he could find jobs, he went out to work for other people. He cooked and washed and ironed and cleaned and scrubbed and whitewashed and beat out rugs.

There wasn't much time for play. Sometimes he would join the colored children in their games for a little while before bedtime. But he was shy and not so strong as the other boys and not much good at rough and tumble sport.

It was only when it came to games of skill that

George could distinguish himself. His bag of marbles swelled and swelled. He had just one agate, but when he rolled it, it always hit the mark. His hand and his eye worked right together. He could throw and hit any mark the boys set.

But mumblety-peg was what the neighborhood admired him most for. When he would fish out his little black-handled knife that he had found in the corn field, all the children gathered around to watch. "Look at that!" they would exclaim as he flipped the blade over his left shoulder while he held on to his right ear. It seemed as if the knife was a live thing and did whatever George told it to.

One day Jim came out to see George.

"Jim, why don't you go to school?" George asked. "You're big and strong. You'll get work in Neosho easy."

Jim came, but he didn't stick to studying long. The plastering work he was learning interested him more than the school. He settled down in the town—he liked it being among his own people.

George liked it, too. He didn't know exactly why, but he was happier in Aunt Mariah's house than he ever had been at the Carvers'. There was more laughter here, more warmth. It was all right to be foolish sometimes. And he could tell Aunt Mariah how he felt about the forest—Uncle Mose and Aunt Sue wouldn't have understood.

There were times when he and Aunt Mariah were very close indeed. That was when he would be reading out of the Bible to her, and they would pray together. It made George feel the way he did in the forest—as if someone was watching over him.

Sometimes they would go to the African Methodist Church together. The preacher there couldn't read, and somebody had to read the Bible for him. But when he talked, George wanted to cry. It seemed as if warm sunshine was pouring over him and melting the tightness in his heart. He thought the preacher must be the best man in the world. Aunt Mariah said he was.

"Of course, Uncle Mose is a very good man, too," George hastened to say. "Why, when one of the neighbors was sick, he helped bring in the hay and the corn for him. And he gave a piece of his own land to be a cemetery for the church people, though he doesn't go to church himself."

"Your Uncle Mose is a good man," Aunt Mariah said. "But he ain't good the same way. He ain't been touched by grace. Now Reverend Givens, he's overflowing with grace; he's all love."

That was it—all love. George wanted to be that way, too.

Aunt Mariah made George a present of a Bible and had him embroider a book mark to keep the place in it. He pored and pored over the book. The part he liked best was where it told about the different plants—how God had made them all for a purpose. He liked to think that God had made everything the way it was for a reason. It made him feel there was a plan for him, too.

By this time George had learned that he was a black boy living in a white world. He understood that the things a white boy could expect to do and be and have a Negro boy could not. White boys could dream of doing exciting and important things, of becoming famous and rich. Colored boys had nothing much to look forward to.

"But if God made everything for a purpose," he thought, "God must have a plan for me, too."

What was that plan?

It certainly couldn't be that he should be sick all his life. Here he was thirteen and not much bigger than when he left home. Maybe like one of his sick plants he needed new soil. Maybe if he went somewhere else where the climate was different he wouldn't feel so weak and tired all the time.

One day he said to Jim, "There's a family moving out to Fort Scott, Kansas. I've been talking with them. They say they'll let me come along if I want to go."

"You going away from Neosho?" Jim asked in surprise. He was very content to stay where he was.

"Maybe I'll feel better out there. Maybe I'll grow some. Maybe there's a school out there I can go to."

Aunt Mariah and Uncle Andy were taken aback when George told them his plan.

"Why, Fort Scott is seventy-five miles away!" Uncle Andy wailed. "We ain't going to see you no more!"

"Now, Andy," Aunt Mariah scolded, "you just stop that. Did the Carvers stand in the way of George's schooling? No! And we ain't going to neither!"

Uncle Andy was silenced and only kept shaking his head in a dismal sort of way. By night time he had thought of something to comfort him. "George," he said, "you write me out a will. You're like a son to me and I'm going to leave you everything."

It made George all warm inside to think people could feel that way about him. Aunt Sue had thought a lot of him, too, and Uncle Mose. He'd go see them before he left for Kansas. He'd carry down that lace collar and cuffs he'd made. And maybe he and Jim could have their picture taken together, and give it to everybody to remember them by, and keep one each themselves.

Fort Scott seemed the end of the world to George. He couldn't quite believe he was going until he saw the wagons piled high with furniture.

"You scared, George?" asked Jim, who had come to see his brother off.

"Reckon I'll get along."

The wagons creaked; the pots and pans jangled.

"Good luck, George!"

"Good-bye, Jim!"

Wanderer

"I HEARD, MA'AM, YOU WANTED SOMEONE TO DO HOUSE-work."

Mrs. Payne, standing at the door of her fine, large house, looked doubtfully at the small, comical looking boy who had knocked. She glanced from George's earnest face with its wide mouth to the long, slim hands. They were so capable looking that in spite of herself she asked, "But do you know how to cook?"

"Yes, ma'am," George answered.

Mrs. Payne continued to look him up and down uncertainly. All at once she made up her mind. "Very well," she said, "I'll give you a chance. But I warn you that my husband is very fussy. Things have to be just so or he won't touch them."

She took George into the kitchen. "You can start dinner now," she said and rattled off the menu.

George's knees grew weak. He knew how to cook, yes, but not these things. Except for the coffee, he had never made any of the dishes the lady had named.

Mrs. Payne seemed not to know he was in trouble. "The towels are in here," she went on briskly, "and the table linen and silver are in the dining room."

"Mrs. Payne!" George was clutching at a straw —he didn't want to be left alone with the pots and pans. "I . . . I . . . I want to do things just like you're used to them. If you show me exactly how you do, I'll be sure to have everything the way you like it."

"That's not a bad idea," Mrs. Payne said unsuspectingly. She put on an apron and began sifting flour for the biscuits.

"I use about so much fat," she said, "and so much baking powder . . . and salt . . . and milk."

George watched how she kneaded the dough, how she rolled it out on the floured board and cut it with a biscuit cutter. When the pan was ready to go into the oven, he drew a deep breath—he was all right now. He knew that if he could see a dish cooked once, he could do it again.

And he did. One by one he got the housewife to show him what she did, and one by one he learned to turn the dishes out better than she could make them herself. He got so expert with his oven that guests could not believe there was only a small boy in the kitchen. When the ladies of Fort Scott held a bread-making contest, it was George who carried off the prizes. Not a single housewife in the town could make such yeast bread, or salt-rising bread, or such yeast and buttermilk batter biscuits.

But George had not left Neosho in order to learn cooking. Cooking was a tool. It was just something to keep his body going while his mind drank in the learning that was in books. As soon as he had saved a little money, he was back in school.

He would take things turn and turn about—work and save for a few weeks, then get in a few weeks of school. He learned what he could, where he could, going wherever chance took him, starting a grade in one small town, finishing it in another.

He did any kind of work that came to hand. He sawed wood, swept yards, did housework. For wherever he went, three insistent questions followed him: Where shall I sleep tonight? Where can I get something to eat? How shall I pay for the books I need?

It was hard. Everything had to come from himself. But George never stopped to think about it—he didn't have time to pity himself. When people were good to him, he was happy. When people were cruel, he went away from them and tried to forget. Alone as he was, he was not lonesome; for always there were the fields and the woods. Under the open sky George was at home.

He would wander along the country roads, and a wonderful feeling would steal over him. How much was in the world to know! Here, for instance, the soil was black, and over there it was yellow or maybe red. Why was that? Plants were the most wonderful things of all. He would dig up a little plant and hold it in his hand and study it. Roots and stem and leaves and flowers—each was made just that way and no other for a purpose. What was the purpose?

Once when George was out walking in the countryside he came to a great wheat field. It was being harvested. Four stout horses were pulling the cutting machine through the wheat, and behind the machine a man was walking. He was binding the wheat. George saw him pick up an armful of the cut wheat, twist a couple of stalks around it and make a knot. The loose wheat became a neat bundle.

"I'd like to do that!" George thought. He ran into the field and started following the bundler.

"What you want, boy?" the bundler asked.

"I want to learn to tie bundles like you're doing."

The man laughed. "Looks easy, don't it?" he said and went on with his work.

George was fascinated. He kept on watching till he had the secret of the knot.

The next day he went boldly up to a farmer and offered himself as a bundler. The farmer couldn't believe a young boy could bundle wheat.

"Let's see you tie a knot," he said.

George swept up an armful of cut wheat, twisted two stalks around it, and tied a knot. The knot stayed tight.

All through that harvest season George bundled wheat. He loved to walk behind the machine and bind. He could do it all day and keep right up with the machine.

There was just one kind of job he liked better than working in the wheat and that was working in a greenhouse. Any time George could get a job in one he was happy. Sometimes, when he had a little money saved up, he would work in a greenhouse for nothing. The fun of handling flowers was pay enough, he thought.

But the chances to work in a greenhouse were few and far between. Most of the time George had to stick to housework of one sort or another. And when he learned to do fine laundry work, washing and ironing became his standby.

It was Mrs. Seymour who taught him that.

Like the Carvers, like the Watkinses, Lucy Seymour and her husband had no children of their own, and their hearts went out to the neat, quiet boy who worked so hard to stay in school. When the barber for whom George had been working moved away, Lucy Seymour took George under her wing.

"You come and be with us, George," she said to him. "That way you can stay in school steady."

So again George had a home. Again there were loving people to say good-morning and good-night to him, regular meals, the same bed night after night. Daytimes now he could study, spare time he could put in helping Mrs. Seymour with her laundry work. His heart was filled with thanks and his hands worked to show what was in his heart.

Temple of Learning

LUCY SEYMOUR HAD BEEN A SLAVE IN A FINE VIRGINIA family and set great store by manners and dress. At the table everything had to be just so. When you walked out of an evening you had to look just so.

She herself was neat as a pin, and on Sundays when she put on her church-going clothes no one would believe that she washed and ironed all week for a living. There would be a snow-white ruff at her neck. Over her neat black dress she would put on a wide collar made of tiny jet beads. And at the back of her head there would be a large tortoise-shell comb. George would try to make himself as neat as he could so that she wouldn't be ashamed of him.

Aunt Mariah had taught George how to wash and iron, and he thought he knew how. But now when Lucy Seymour took him in hand, he realized he was just an amateur. Lucy Seymour was known as the best shirt ironer and polisher in the country.

She took great pains to teach her art to George. First she taught him how to do up shirts. When he had mastered that, she let him go on to fancy dresses and underskirts. When George got so that he could turn out an underskirt so stiff with starch that it would stand up by itself, Lucy Seymour said he was ready to graduate.

George laughed, but he kept her words in mind. One day he said, "Well, Mrs. Seymour, I think I really will graduate. What would you say if I opened up a laundry?"

"Where, George?" Mrs. Seymour asked.

"Right here in town. I've got my eye on a little one-room house on Main Street. It's got a kitchen lean-to. It would be just fine for a laundry," George said.

Mrs. Seymour didn't want him to bite off more

than he could chew. "How much is the house?" she asked.

"A hundred and fifty dollars. But I wouldn't have to pay it all at once," he added hastily. "The man told me I could pay five dollars a month."

"Well, then, try," said Lucy Seymour.

So George went into the laundry business in the town of Minneapolis, Kansas. A stove to heat water, a boiler, a couple of tubs, a washboard, rope and pins, soap, starch, blueing, an ironing board, a bit of candle, a couple of irons, and he was set.

Now he felt that he had really grown up. As he stood over his washtubs or ironing board, as he carried heavy baskets of wash through the streets, he felt that he really had his feet on the ground. He had worked hard at his books. He was getting close to his goal—a little more and he would be ready for college!

He was thinking a great deal about college now. In the town of Highland there was a university. It was just a small place with not quite a hundred students. But for that very reason George fixed on it. He would have a better chance, he thought, to get in there—they might not be so fussy about what he knew and didn't know.

So George wrote a letter. It was the most important letter he had ever written and he worded it very carefully and signed it George W. Carver. Some time before, he had given himself the middle initial because there was another George Carver in town and their mail sometimes got mixed.

"What does the *W* stand for? Washington?" someone asked him.

George smiled and said yes, that's what it was—George Washington Carver. What difference did it make? he thought. It might as well be Washington as anything else. Did it matter what middle name a boy had when he was an orphan and didn't even know when his birthday was?

On the day a letter finally came saying that the university would be happy to have him, George didn't get much work done. He read his letter over about a hundred times.

"Now my years of wandering are over," he said happily to himself. "Now the road will no longer twist and turn for me. I will go straight ahead—up and up and up."

Through all the years in which George had scurried around trying to pick up a crumb of knowledge here and another crumb there, he had carried a certain picture in the back of his mind. It was a picture out of the old Webster's blue-back Speller that Aunt

Sue had given him. The picture showed a man climbing a high cliff. On the top of the cliff stood a temple of learning. George had always thought of himself as that man and the temple of learning as his goal. Now he was about to set foot on the lowest step of the temple!

It never occurred to him to worry about how he would work his way through college—he had always worked his way through school. He would get along. In fact, he was better off now than he had ever been before. For one thing, he wasn't sick and puny any more. All of a sudden he had started to grow and had shot up to six feet.

"I'll sell my laundry," George told Lucy Seymour. "And this summer I'll take a trip till school opens."

Not long before, he had learned that Jim had died of smallpox. George wanted to visit his brother's grave and to see the Carvers and Aunt Mariah and all the other people who had been good to him back home in Missouri. He hadn't seen them for thirteen years, not since he left Neosho. How proud they would be of their George when he told them he was going to enter college!

That summer, in which he said good-bye to his childhood, seemed to George the longest of his life. But it passed at last and the opening day came. In a fever of excitement George arrived at the university. Tall and straight and smiling, he stood in his neat, gray checked suit in front of the principal's desk and waited.

The gentleman looked up. "Well, what do you want?" he asked sharply. He was busy.

"I am George W. Carver, sir. I've come to attend the university."

The principal stared. Then he frowned and shook his head. "We take only Indians here—no Negroes," he said curtly and returned to his papers.

The smile died on George's face. He started to say something, changed his mind, turned slowly, and stumbled through the door.

All the joy had gone out of the world.

Kansas Pioneer

8

GEORGE HAD OFTEN BEEN HURT BEFORE. PEOPLE HAD taunted him and stormed and sworn at him on account of his skin. In a hundred ways they had tried to make him feel that because he was a Negro he was not quite human. Invisible fences were all around him. You can't go here. You can't eat with us. This is only for white folks.

He had learned to take the hurts and hide them,

though sometimes he felt it would be easier to be a mule—a mule could feel only blows to his body. "Why do you care?" he would say to himself when he wanted to cry. "If they don't want you, you don't want them."

But this new bar was too much. Slowly, one small step at a time, he had struggled up the cliff. And now, when he had almost reached the temple door, it had been shut in his face.

"Why? Why?" he asked himself. "What difference does the color of my skin make? I don't want to change it; all I want is to learn."

George was very miserable. Hope, that had never left him before, left him now.

With dragging feet he started to look for work. He didn't want to sweep yards and beat rugs and wash and iron other people's clothes any more. So long as that kind of work had put him a step ahead towards college, he didn't mind doing it. But now that his dream was over, now that he saw only a lifetime of dull, hard work ahead of him, work lost its meaning.

To his surprise George found that in this town he didn't have to look for work—work was looking for him. He didn't know that people were putting jobs in his way. The story of how the college had turned the Negro boy away had got out, and a number of ladies felt indignant.

Mrs. Beeler was the most indignant of all.

"Highland College was started by our church, John," she said to her husband. "I feel ashamed to think it isn't acting up to the principles it teaches. I'm going to take that young man in and let him help me around the house."

The Beelers had a fruit farm outside the town. At another time George would have loved being there, but now it didn't seem to matter. He couldn't throw off his gloom. Once in a while when he would be out in the orchard, he would try. "I've got to get hold of myself," he would say. "I can't just let myself drift —I've got to make my life count for something." But the hurt was stronger than he was. All he seemed to want to do was run away.

Mrs. Beeler came very near understanding him. One day she said to him, "George, you need to get away. Go and do something new. Run if you want to run, but run *towards* something, not just *away*. That's what I said to my boy, Frank. And that's what I am saying to you."

George thought about it. Frank Beeler had gone out as a homesteader to western Kansas, to the Great

American Desert. The Government was giving the land away free to anyone who would go out and live on it for five years. Frank had taken up some of this free land. He had built a store out there and started a town. He had given the town his own name—Beeler.

"Well, why not?" George thought. "I'll get some government land and make a farm. The Government won't ask what color my skin is."

So he went. Two miles south of Beeler he found free land. He filed for 160 acres and settled down to be a homesteader.

He was prepared to rough it. But even George, who had roughed it all his life, was surprised to find how rough pioneering in western Kansas could be.

On his hundred and sixty acres he was alone. Everything that needed to be done had to be done by his own hands. The desert prairie stretched out all around him as far as eye could see. Neither hills nor rocks broke the flatness. There were no roads. There were no trees—the nearest were a clump of poplars thirty miles away. There was nothing here but sky and buffalo grass and yucca and cactus. He was alone with the land and the sky.

"Reckon a house to live in is the first thing," George decided.

He had taken a good look at the sod houses in Beeler and had been foresighted enough to bring to his acres everything he would need to build himself a home. With his plow he cut the buffalo sod evenly into strips four inches thick and a foot wide. He cut each strip into two foot lengths. Then he laid the pieces out in a hollow square and set them one on top of another like bricks. Over his wooden ridge pole and rafters he also laid sod. And on top of the sod he piled dirt until the roof was a foot thick.

A good many of the houses he had seen had stopped when they got as far as this. But George wasn't satisfied. He raked the roof off smoothly and trimmed the walls down inside with a sharp spade. Then, to keep the dirt from sifting into his house, he whitewashed the inside walls with lime. Later on, he thought, after he got his crops in, he would plant flowers around his soddy.

"Now," thought George, "if only my crops turn out all right, I'll be a farmer for fair. Maybe that is the plan for me."

He was living closer to nature than he had ever done, and he liked it, even though he missed the trees that meant so much to him. He would throw his head back and look and look at the immense dome of the blue sky that came down like a bowl over the land.

At night he would look up and gasp to see the brightness of a thousand stars.

Sometimes there would be the aurora borealis to look at. George thought of all wonders that was the most wonderful. He would stretch out on the ground and watch for hours while the sheets and columns of colored light shimmered and faded and gleamed again.

Sometimes in the early morning or in the late afternoon he would see a mirage. That was almost as wonderful and even more mysterious. Right ahead of him he would suddenly see a lake with a ship and people on it. Or perhaps a stream would suddenly appear in which people were fishing or canoeing.

The weather here was different from any he had known, and George watched it first with interest—and afterwards with dismay. The spring was lovely. The desert grew green, the corn came up tall and straight. But then came the hot winds. Everything wilted under their blast. No rain, no shade came weeks on end.

In the winter there were the blizzards. George was working part time on a livestock ranch that joined his own property when he met the first one. He had never seen anything like it, though he had seen snow storms aplenty.

"George," the ranch owner said to him one day,

"I've got to go to Larned to get supplies and may not be back for a week. You get the stock in under cover every night while I'm gone. There may be a blizzard."

It was a beautiful, bright day, about thirty below zero, and a blizzard seemed to be the last thing to expect.

"A blizzard, Mr. Steeley?" George asked, surprised.

"Yes, and I mean blizzard. When you get the stock in, see that you stay in yourself. Don't dare to go out! Don't go out for anything!"

George felt insulted. He didn't like being talked to as if he was a child.

"I've seen blizzards before," he said.

"No, you haven't, George. You've seen storms, but not blizzards. Mind me now and stay in."

In this treeless country people used sunflower stalks and sun-dried cow dung for fuel. The day after Mr. Steeley left, George was out with a team getting cow-chips when about two o'clock in the afternoon he noticed a strange little strip of bluish cloud on the horizon. By three o'clock the strip had grown a yard wide.

"Can that be a blizzard coming?" George wondered.

Quickly he started rounding up the stock. It took about an hour to do that, and by the time he was through, the curious strip of cloud had grown very wide. It began to snow.

A half hour later it was snowing very hard. George was standing by the window with his nose to the pane. But all he could see was swirling snow. The barn, which was less than a hundred yards away, had disappeared just as if it had been swallowed up.

All of a sudden George felt a terrible desire to experience the storm at first hand. He just had to see what it was like to be out in a blizzard. He had heard that in this country people sometimes got lost in a blizzard right in their own back yard. Sometimes, he had been told, people were found frozen to death a few feet from their own door. Could such things really be true?

He would find out. He got a rope, tied one end to a bed post and, holding tight to the other end, opened the door and stepped out.

The wind tore at him as if he were an enemy. It whistled and blew the snow furiously about. Though it was only around five in the afternoon, the darkness was so deep and the snow so thick that George could see nothing of the farm buildings. He put his hand up in front of his face. Six inches away he could not see his hand. He took three or four steps forward and turned to look at the house. The blizzard had swallowed it!

George struggled inside and bolted the door. He knew what a blizzard was now!

Summer and winter George was learning by hard experience that the desert was not an easy country to live in. "If things just depended on me," he often thought, "I could make a go of it. I'm not afraid of work, and what the next man can do, I can do. But this weather. . . ."

Gradually George had to accept the fact that he had made a mistake. Try as he would, he could not make farming in the desert pay. This was grazing country, not farm land. He knew he could never last out the five years he must stay to own his 160 acres. Besides, he missed the trees. He was hungry for the kind of country he had always known. He had run away here, but now he could not wait to run back.

Yet he was not sorry he had come. Living close to the land and the sky like this had been good for him, and he knew it. Little by little his spirit had healed. He was able to work at his books again. He was able to paint again. He began to dream again about the temple of learning.

Another Dream Comes True

ON A DAY IN SEPTEMBER IN THE YEAR 1890 A MAN walked along the dusty Iowa road leading to the town of Indianola. In one hand he carried a shabby satchel. In the other he had a box through the open top of which some strange-looking cactus plants could be seen. He had been walking for twenty-five miles and had often stopped to rest. But there was spring in his step now; for he was getting near the end of his journey.

People meeting the young man glanced at him curiously. Where on earth was this Negro going with his battered satchel and his cactus plants?

They would have stared harder if they had known that George was bound for Simpson College. They would have been even more astonished if they could read the thoughts in his mind.

In about an hour he was going to find out if Simpson College would let him in. If the answer was "yes," he knew what he would do with his life. He would study painting. He would prove by becoming an artist that talent had nothing to do with the color of a person's skin. He would show the whole world that a Negro could do anything a white man could.

In after years George often wondered what would have happened if President Holmes had said "no." At that time George was too busy answering questions to think about it. What had he studied? Where?

George had a hard time remembering. He was thirty years old now. He had been to so many schools in so many places, a few weeks here, a few weeks there. Much of what he knew he hadn't learned in school at all. He had got it out of books on his own, had dug it out of a library, had heard it at a lecture, had learned it in the woods.

Dr. Holmes listened, and as he listened, his respect grew. But there were rules.

"You have not had enough mathematics," he said at last. "You will have to come in as a special student."

"That's all right, sir."

George didn't care. All he wanted was to be allowed to study, on any terms. He was in—that was the important thing—they had not turned him away. Carefully he counted out twelve dollars for his tuition.

The fact that he had just ten cents left didn't bother him too much. He was used to having his purse empty. Besides, Dr. Holmes had said he could live in an old abandoned shack belonging to the college; so his main problem was solved. Ten cents, he reckoned, would see him through the first week's food. Things for his laundry he would get on credit.

As he carried his satchel and his cactus plants down to the shack, George had a lighter heart than in years. What did it matter that he would be far from the campus? He was lucky to have anything at all. He put his things inside the hut, shut the door, and walked over to the main street to buy on credit the two wash tubs, the board, irons, soap, and starch he would need. The question of food was simple. In a grocery store he bought five cents' worth of corn meal. In a butcher shop he spent his last five cents on beef suet.

"My big problem," George thought as he lugged his purchases home, "is a stove. I'll have to try a junk shop for that—it would cost too much anywhere else." And he went out again.

In a little while he was back with a small stove he had bought for a few cents' credit. He had also picked up a battered black pan that someone had thought too bad to use and had thrown into an ash can. The kindly junk dealer had made him a present of a badly dented wash boiler, but George decided he would go back for that next day. What he needed right now was a couple of boxes to serve as table and chair. He would sleep on the floor until he could stop to build himself a bed.

George had so often before solved the problems of how to get food and where to sleep that he made his arrangements almost without wasting a motion. All the while he was setting up his home and laundry, he was actually puzzling over something else. This something else seemed to him much more difficult to solve.

Simpson College had let him in, and, of course, he

was grateful for that. But it wasn't letting him study what he wanted.

"Art?" the authorities had echoed in amazement. "Why, that's ridiculous. Who ever heard of a colored person wanting to study art? What for? Don't you realize you should be studying something you can make a living at?"

George had given in, but only for the time. As he washed out the black pan and put a little corn meal on to soak, he said to himself, "I won't give up, I can't. I'll tackle them again. I'll get around them somehow."

The next day the first thing George did was to find the art room.

Ever since he had read about it in the college catalog, George had imagined to himself that "elegant room immediately under the skylight." The vision of that room had kept step with him all the way along the road to Indianola. Now he found it even finer than he had imagined.

For a little while he stood outside looking longingly through the door. Then the sight of easels and brushes and people painting became too much for him. He got his courage up and walked over to the art director. All night long he had been thinking out what he would say and now he blurted it out.

"Miss Budd, don't you think that if a person has talent for art he should develop it?"

The teacher looked up confused. She had already heard about the young colored fellow who wanted to study art. Along with the rest she agreed that it wasn't a practical thing for a Negro to do. But George's question put her on the spot.

"Yes, I do," she admitted honestly. "However," she added, looking very hard at him, "he has to be *sure* he has talent!"

George had his answer ready. "Well, Miss Budd, how can I find out whether I have talent if I don't try?"

Miss Budd flushed. She was cornered. She had to admit George had a point.

"Very well," she said reluctantly. "You can come to class for two weeks. At the end of that time I'll tell you whether you have any talent."

With that George had to be content.

Laundryman-Artist

10

HOW GEORGE ENVIED THE YOUNG LADIES WHO COULD study art whether they had any talent or not!

They seemed to take their work as a matter of course. They sat before their easels and chatted and laughed while they painted and sketched. As for George, he sat silent and tense. Miss Budd had set him to copying a drawing of wooden figures, and he was all in a sweat over it. He didn't like to copy. He could paint flowers from Nature or from memory, but copying was something he could see no sense in. Would she be satisfied with the way he was doing the shading?

As the two weeks drew to an end and Miss Budd said nothing, George grew more and more disturbed. He waited and he waited. Finally he could stand it no longer. After class he went up to the desk.

"Please, Miss Budd!"

"Yes?"

"You said that if I showed any talent, I could stay in the class. May I?"

"I don't see why not," Miss Budd said briefly. "You may start doing landscapes."

She said this so half-heartedly that George wondered whether Miss Budd really believed he was talented. He couldn't guess that she spoke that way only because she was so troubled about him. In the first few days she had seen that he was gifted. "But I haven't any right," she kept saying to herself, "to encourage a Negro to go into art when there's no practical sense in it!"

If her words sounded half-hearted to George, the smile with which she followed them was not. All of a sudden he found himself confiding his troubles.

"Miss Budd," he said, "I had hoped by this time that I would have money enough to pay for the art course. But I haven't. I haven't any money at all. Dr. Holmes said he would ask the students to bring me their laundry to do. I guess he forgot."

Something about George warned Miss Budd, "Don't offer money. He will be offended if you do." But she wanted so very much to help this promising and likable young man!

"Could you saw some wood?" she asked, thinking fast. "I need to have some stove wood cut. You can saw it for the tuition if you like."

In the back of her mind a still better plan was forming.

A couple of days later George heard a knock on his door, and on opening it found a lady standing there. She smiled in a friendly way, quite as though she knew him.

"I am an old pupil of Miss Budd's," she said as if that explained everything. "Mrs. Liston is my name."

"Yes, ma'am," George said politely and waited.

For a moment Mrs. Liston didn't seem to know what she wanted. She had come because Miss Budd had asked her to help George get a decent place to stay. But when she saw him, she realized at once that she couldn't say that. She would have to turn things the other way around—pretend that she needed George to help her instead.

"I . . . I . . . I would like to paint my garden," she stammered, then went on quickly. "But my drawing is not good enough. Miss Budd thought you might help me with it."

George's face lit up. "I would be delighted to do it, ma'am," he said.

While they arranged the time, Mrs. Liston's eyes took in the old stove, the empty boiler, the pan half full of corn meal and water.

"I know of a much better place for your laundry," she said when the right moment came. "Some friends of mine have a room you could have—it's opposite the canning factory. It would be much closer than this to the college."

After that visit things happened fast. Mrs. Liston buzzed around, said a few words here, a few words there, and laundry began to pour in on George. The hard times were over.

Friendship came right along with the washing. The boys who brought their shirts to George found they wanted to stay and talk. For this young man who decorated his bare room with cactus plants and amaryllis, this young man who held a book in one hand while he stirred boiling clothes with the other, had fascinating things to tell. In twenty years of wandering George had picked up all kinds of information.

The boys liked to hear his adventures. And they liked his talk about the out-of-doors—he could make anybody curious about rocks and plants. On Saturday and Sunday afternoons when George went to walk in the woods, there was always a bunch of boys who wanted to go along.

George was older than the other students, but it didn't seem to matter. The boys couldn't find enough ways to show how much they thought of him. One would slip a ticket to a lecture under his door. Another would push through a fifty cent piece. And George could never find out who did these things; whenever he accused someone, the person always said, "Not me!"

George got very used to hearing "Not me!" One day he came back to his room to find it transformed—for a moment he thought he was in the wrong place. Instead of the rough table and chair he had made out of boxes, there was a whole set of comfortable furniture—bed, table, chairs, dresser. The boys had clubbed together and bought the things for him. But when he asked, he got nothing but "Not me!" for an answer.

Whatever the students were doing, they wanted George to be in on it. It was always, "Come along, George!" They wanted him on their baseball team, in their concerts, in their choir, in their school clubs. They made him feel that his color made no difference. George for the first time in his life felt what it was like to have no invisible fences around him. It was like coming into the sunlight after being underground.

Something inside him melted, grew warm, glowed. Oh, he was happy, happy, happy. For the first time he could think of himself as a human being just like anybody else. "People don't expect any more or any less of me than of any other human being," he thought.

But just because of this, George longed to stand on his tiptoes and make his life count for something. "I have God's work to do," he told himself, "I have my people to serve." The only question in his mind was how he could serve them best.

Was it through art?

Beyond everything else in the world George loved his painting. Now that he was allowed to work on whatever he liked, he was wonderfully at peace in the art room. And Miss Budd was content, too. Chance and a painting of red roses had shown her that she had every right to encourage George.

The roses were another student's. Alice had fussed and fussed over them for weeks, but all her fussing seemed to get her nowhere. Every brush stroke only made the roses look worse. They looked so much like a daub of red paint that even Miss Budd finally lost patience.

"I'm afraid, Alice, you have no talent," she had said sharply and had gone out of the art room.

George was the only person left with unhappy Alice. He sat before his easel wishing he could have a chance to paint red roses instead of this green sea he was doing. It would be a very long time before Miss Budd would let him do red roses.

All of a sudden he heard Alice exclaim, "I can't do it!" and throw down her brush. She was ready to cry.

George walked over. "Here," he said, "let me help."

With quick, sure strokes he began to paint. And immediately the red daub turned into roses. The flowers stood out from the canvas, the petals curled as rose petals should, the light and shadow played in the right places. Before Alice's startled eyes her painting came to life.

They were both so excited about what was happening that they forgot all about Miss Budd. Then they heard her footsteps in the hall. George dropped the brush and backed away just as she came in.

Miss Budd's eye fell instantly on the picture. She

stopped short, stared, then came close. She couldn't believe this had happened in the hour she was away.

"Alice," she exclaimed enthusiastically, "that's the best work I've seen you do! I really believe you've caught the spirit of it at last!"

Alice threw George a glance, then both started laughing.

"It isn't mine," Alice explained, shamefaced. "George did it."

After that George was allowed to paint flowers to his heart's content. Yucca, roses, peonies, amaryllis —any flower he had ever seen he could bring to life on canvas. He made flowers so real, people wanted to lean over and smell them.

But what could he do with this talent? The question bothered Miss Budd even more than it did George. She somehow felt responsible.

One afternoon toward the end of the year they were in the art room together talking. As usual it was about George's career.

"You will never be able to earn a living at painting flowers," Miss Budd said, just as she had done many times before.

"I'm afraid you are right," George answered gloomily, just as he had done many times before.

"If only we could think of something that would

bring all your talents together," Miss Budd continued. "You love art and you love Nature. What does that add up to?"

"There is a man at the United States Department of Agriculture who makes wax fruit. Maybe I could do something like that," George suggested.

Miss Budd sniffed. "That will never do for you," she said firmly. "You've got to do something bigger, George."

"Art is very big," George said. He was clinging as hard as he could to his painting.

"Yes, art is very big," Miss Budd agreed. "But the question is: Is it big enough for you, for what you want to do? You tell me you are going back to your people in the South. You say you want to help open their minds. Do you think you can do it by bringing them paintings?"

George looked silently out of the art room windows and thought about the millions of his people just freed from slavery. They were so poor, so ignorant. In his heart he knew that painting was not what they needed. They needed to learn how to live, how to work, how to think—as free human beings.

"George," Miss Budd said earnestly, "it's not that I want you to give up painting. You must never give it up. But you must paint for pleasure, not for a living. What would you think of developing your other great interest—Nature?"

"How?" George asked.

"Well, there's agricultural science. Most of your people in the South are farmers. Yet they know nothing about the soil, nothing about scientific farming. If you brought them science. . . ."

Miss Budd broke off. Both she and George remained for a long time silent, thinking. At last Miss Budd spoke.

"I know it's hard, George," she said gently. "But I think in the end you won't be sorry if you lay aside your brushes. Listen now. My father is a scientist. He works with garden plants. He is Professor of Horticulture at the Iowa State Agricultural College. Supposing I write to him. . . ."

"Cast Down Your Bucket!"

11

YEARS PASS QUICKLY WHEN YOU ARE HAPPY, AND AT Iowa State George was very happy.

"I was wise to switch over to agriculture," he told himself as he got more and more interested in botany and chemistry. "Miss Budd was right—I don't regret it."

Once in a while, to be sure, as the years passed George still daydreamed: "Wouldn't it be wonderful to study art in Paris!" But not even when one of his paintings got an honorable mention at the Chicago World's Fair would he change his mind.

And now here he was with college behind him and getting to the end of his first year on a real job. Good-bye forever to laundryman and houseboy and janitor and cook! He was Assistant Botanist at the Iowa Agricultural Experiment Station. He had done so well in his studies that the college hadn't wanted to let him go.

Once George had thought nothing so much fun as working in a greenhouse. Now he could spend all day six days a week, if he liked, working in the finest greenhouse in Iowa.

"And for the finest boss in the world, too," George told everybody. "That's what Professor Wilson is."

On Saturday and Sunday afternoons, just as he had done at Simpson, George would go rambling. The nine hundred acre campus was a world in itself, but often he would go far beyond it. He loved this prosperous Iowa country. Every farm had a good, solid house. Every barn and silo was painted and well kept. Sleek cattle cropped the lush, green grass. Hogs and turkeys and chickens were part of every farm. In the fertile fields clever machines made the work easier for the farmer.

George would look at the prosperity about him,

and his heart would fill with joy. But there were times when all the richness and plenty only cast him down. For he knew that very soon now he must be going. Aunt Mariah had said, "Don't keep your learning just for yourself—give it all back to your people." The time was fast approaching when he would have to keep faith with Aunt Mariah.

Where would the Call come from? Where would he go? Often and often George would name the Southern states over to himself and wonder, "Which one?"

But while he wondered, the wheels of fate were turning. Something was going on in the South that would answer the question he was asking. Sometimes things that are happening hundreds of miles away and seem to have no connection with us are the very ones that shape our lives.

In the fall of 1895 the city of Atlanta, Georgia was buzzing with excitement. The Cotton States were just about ready to open their Exposition, and everybody in the city was keyed up. Every Southerner felt he had a part in the Exposition. Most of them felt as if they themselves were going to be on display.

For people from all over America and the world were coming to see how the South had "come back." The South was going to show everybody that it hadn't been licked by the Civil War. No, sir! It had pulled itself up by its bootstraps and in thirty years had made a lot of progress. People were going to see how well the white men of the South had got along without slaves. They were also going to see what slaves had done as free men. A Negro Building—designed by a Negro, built every bit by Negro mechanics, and filled with exhibits of Negro work—was part of the Exposition.

On the opening day the great hall in which the speeches were going to be made was packed with thousands of people—white and black. Outside, thousands more who couldn't get in were milling around. Many crowded around the open windows—perhaps something of what was going to be said would drift through to them.

On the platform sat the speakers. Governor Bullock was there, Bishop Nelson of Georgia was there, also the President of the Exposition, and the President of the Women's Board, and a whole row of other important people. Among all the white faces on the platform, there was just one black one. It drew every eye like a magnet.

Everybody knew who the Negro was. The papers had been full of the fact that Booker T. Washington,

Principal of the Tuskegee Normal and Industrial School in Alabama, had been invited to speak on the opening day. Some of the papers were for it. Some were against—they didn't think a Negro should be allowed to speak from the same platform as white men and women. Certainly not on a great national occasion such as this. It never had happened before.

How did he feel, people wondered, that Negro, sprung up from slavery? Sitting up there with all those important white people, how did he feel? Was he nervous? He was going to speak to the richest and best educated people of the South. Among them there would be perhaps even his former masters. At the same time he was going to speak to people from the North, men and women who had helped to set the Negroes free. And he was going to speak to the colored men who were his brothers.

What was he going to say?

All the time the other speakers were making their addresses, the audience sat tense. It was waiting, waiting, waiting for the black man to speak.

At last he rose. The audience could see now that he was tall and very straight, with a high forehead and piercing eyes.

"Mr. President and Gentlemen of the Board of Directors and Citizens," he began in a rich, deep voice. "One-third of the population of the South is of the Negro race."

Every eye was on him, every ear was straining to hear. In the great hall not a sound except the speaker's voice could be heard. In words something like this he went on:

"No enterprise to make life better in the South can fully succeed if it leaves the Negro out. The fact that the Negro has not been left out here, at this Exposition, will do more to strengthen the friendship of the two races than anything that has happened since the dawn of Negro freedom.

"There is a story I should like to tell you:

"A ship was many days lost at sea. All its water was gone, the sailors were mad with thirst. Suddenly they sighted a friendly vessel. Immediately a signal was sent from the mast: 'Water, water; we die of thirst!'

"The answer from the friendly vessel at once came back: 'Cast down your bucket where you are!'

"The Captain could not understand. Were they to drink salt water? He ordered the signal to be sent again: 'Water, water; send us water!'

"Again the answer came: 'Cast down your bucket where you are.'

"Surely there must be some mistake! A third and a fourth time the answer came back: 'Cast down your bucket where you are.'

"At last the Captain heeded the message. He cast down his bucket—and it came up full of fresh, sparkling water from the mouth of the Amazon River."

The speaker paused. A ripple passed over the audience—people were not sure they understood. Why had Washington told that story?

"There are those of my race," the speaker went on, "who think to go to a foreign land to better their condition. There are those who think it is not very important to make a friend of the Southern white man who is their next-door neighbor. To them I would say: 'Cast down your bucket where you are. Cast it down in making friends in every manly way of the people of all races by whom we are surrounded. Cast it down in farming, mechanics, in business, in domestic service, and in the professions."

Now they understood. The audience hung on every word.

"There are those of the white race," the speaker continued, "who also look abroad. They want people of foreign birth to come in and bring prosperity to the South. To them I would repeat what I say to my own race: 'Cast down your bucket where you are.'

"Cast it down among the eight millions of Negroes who have tilled your fields and cleared your forests. They have built your railroads and cities. They have brought forth treasures from the bowels of the earth. They have helped make possible this Exposition of the progress of the South. Cast your bucket down among these people. They are the most patient, faithful, law-abiding, unresentful people that the world has seen.

"Help them to make the most of themselves. Help them to become useful and intelligent citizens. Help them, and it will pay a thousand percent."

He swept his eyes over the sea of faces. He could not read their expression. All he saw was that he had attention. The thousands of eyes were fixed upon him.

"We march side by side," he said. "Nearly sixteen millions of hands will aid you in pulling the load upward, or they will pull against you downward. We can be one-third and more of the ignorance and crime of the South, or we can be one-third of its intelligence and progress.

"God has laid a great and difficult problem at the doors of the South. I promise you that in working it out you shall have the patient help of my race.

"Thirty years ago both of us started with practically nothing. Let us work towards prosperity together. And while we do that, perhaps we can win to something yet more important. Perhaps we can blot out race hatred and suspicion. So will we bring to our beloved South a new heaven and a new earth."

Wild applause broke out as the speaker returned to his seat. People clapped and stamped and shouted and wept. The Governor rushed across the platform to shake hands with Washington.

"It was wonderful, wonderful!" he exclaimed. "You've struck just the right note. We shall all cast down our buckets where we are!"

The Governor said it, fine gentlemen and ladies said it, poor, ignorant Negroes said it. Everywhere the words "Cast down your bucket where you are" sounded like a never-ending echo.

Next day newspapers all over the country carried Booker T. Washington's speech on their front pages. Up in New England friends of the Negro people read it. In New York, Chicago, San Francisco people read it. In New Orleans, St. Louis, Kansas City people read it.

At the Iowa Agricultural Experiment Station, George Washington Carver read it. He was ready to cast his bucket down.

The Call

12

"PROFESSOR WILSON, CAN YOU GIVE ME A FEW MINutes?"

"Come in, Carver, come in!"

George shut the door of the Director's office and took a chair on the other side of the desk. The professor saw that his Assistant Botanist was disturbed about something.

"I received this letter an hour ago," George said, passing an envelope across the desk.

"From Tuskegee, Alabama!" Wilson examined the postmark with surprise, then began to read.

He took a long time over the letter. When he laid it down, his face was grave. "I can see by your manner, Carver," he said, "that you have already made up your mind to accept."

"I don't think I can hesitate, sir."

For a little while Professor Wilson didn't say anything. He just drummed with his fingers on the table. But the shrewd, kindly face of the Scotchman showed how disappointed he was. In the four years George had been a student at the Iowa State Agricultural College they had grown very close. This past year, working together at the Experiment Station, Professor Wilson had come to regard him almost as a son.

"I don't want to go against your conscience, Carver," the Director said at last. "I will not speak about what it will mean to me personally if you leave—except to say one thing: I will never part from any other student with so much regret."

"Thank you, sir. I . . ."

"I know, Carver," Professor Wilson interrupted. "I know how you feel. But do you quite realize what it will mean to the Station if you go? It will be difficult—impossible—to fill your place."

George opened his mouth to speak, but the professor stopped him with a wave of his hand.

"It's nonsense to deny it," he said. "No one I have ever seen has such a passion for plants as you. No one is such an observer, such a collector. Those fungi you got together; you must have some 20,000 specimens, I should judge—molds, mildews, toadstools, and all. Add to that that you understand soils. You are also very expert in grafting. And about cross-breeding plants to create new varieties you know as much as any professor here—and more."

Professor Wilson paused. Then he concluded in a tone full of regret, "I had planned, Carver, that you should work with fruit trees and plants from all over the world. I had hoped you would select and breed new kinds for the farmers and fruit growers of Iowa."

George got up and started pacing up and down the room. It was hard for him to hear the opportunities he would miss.

"There is also the question of salary, Carver," Professor Wilson added. "You will receive more here than Tuskegee is offering you. Fifteen hundred dollars a year isn't much."

George stopped short in his pacing. "It is not a consideration with me, sir," he said and sat down again.

"I expected you would say that—it's like you. But tell me this. What makes you want to go to Tuskegee so much? You have had another, and a better, offer that would take you down among your people."

George tried to put his feelings into words.

"I believe, Professor," he said slowly, "it is because I see eye to eye with Mr. Washington—I have been much moved by his Atlanta speech. . . . I believe we could work together toward the same end."

George looked away out of the window as he spoke. It was almost as though he were thinking aloud.

"It has always been the one great ideal of my life," he went on earnestly, "to be of the greatest good to the greatest number of my people possible. I took up agriculture because I feel that it is the key that will open the door of freedom for my people. You can see from his letter that Mr. Washington feels the same way about it. I think that a school headed by him would have a spirit in which my work would count for most."

"A spirit of service," Wilson said thoughtfully.

George nodded. "I am sure," he said, "that with Washington as head, the students would be filled with the desire to serve. Each of them would feel it his duty to go back to the district from which he came and pass on to others what he learned from me. What

I taught would spread far and always farther."

George reached out for the letter and put it in the inner pocket of his jacket. There was a sweet pea in his button hole—he never was without a flower—and he took care not to hurt it.

"I've been thinking, too," he said, "that I should like to reach out beyond the school to the whole county. I want to tackle the soil problem. It is the great problem of the South."

"You yourself would have a great deal to learn, Carver," Professor Wilson said. "The region will be new to you."

"I know that, sir. I'll learn."

Professor Wilson stretched out his hand across the desk. "Our loss will be the South's gain," he said. "I recognize the finger of Providence and I submit."

"It is a great opportunity," George said simply as he shook the outstretched hand and got up to go. "I take it as a Call, sir."

"Where Shall I Begin?"

13

GOING DOWN ON THE TRAIN TO TUSKEGEE, GEORGE Carver was all eyes. He had read and read about cotton, but he had never seen it. Now it was everywhere around him. Fields of coppery stalks and puffs of white slipped endlessly by the window. And here and there in the fields he could see the people of King Cotton's kingdom.

It was early October, cotton picking time. Everybody who could raise a hand to pick was in the fields.

Backs bent a little above the rows, black hands reached for the white fluff. As the train passed, the backs would straighten for a moment, the hands hold still. The pickers looked curiously at the monster roaring through the cotton. And from the train window Carver looked curiously back at them.

"Cotton—that's all they know," he thought. "Cotton—that's all their life."

Whenever he caught sight of the miserable, unpainted shacks in which the people lived, his heart sank. Every roof sagged in the middle. The falling chimneys were propped by sticks. There wasn't a tree to give shade, there wasn't a flower in the dooryard. Once in a while a little patch of corn or sugar cane would appear near a cabin. But much more often the cotton came right up to the door—the cabin looked lost in the cotton.

The memory of Uncle Mose Carver's farm rose before him. That was a one-room house, too. But it wasn't like these shacks. He thought of the horses and the cows, the sheep and the poultry. He recalled the beehives and the fruit trees.

"Uncle Mose and Aunt Sue raised almost everything they needed," he thought. "They lived well, they had plenty. But these people raise nothing but cotton; so how can they live well? What do they eat?"

His heart sank even more when he saw the worn-out and wasted land. In many fields the cotton was stunted and bore very few white puffs. In others, because the top soil had been washed away, nothing would grow at all. The rolling country lay utterly bare, wrinkled and scarred with deep gullies.

Carver knew the reason for that. King Cotton had ruled over the South too long. Cotton had been planted on the same acres over and over again until all the good had been taken out of the soil. Then forests had been cut down to make more land for cotton. Once the trees were gone, there was nothing to hold the rain water. It ran off the surface, taking the top soil along with it.

"I can help my people only by healing their sick land," Carver thought. "And I can heal this sick land only through the people. It goes around in a circle like that. Where am I to begin?"

The problem was so big. What he saw out of the train window was just a tiny part of the cotton belt. If he traveled east and west for a thousand miles, he would see the same dirty, unpainted shacks, the same rain-gullied fields, the same straggling fences. Everywhere he would find the people just as poor, just as ill fed. They would be wearing the same jeans and dresses made out of feed bags. They would be doing the same drudging, monotonous work. He would find no flowers in their yards, no beauty or comfort in their houses.

"Where am I to begin?"

The question throbbed in his brain. He heard it in the rattle of the wheels. It sounded in the whistle of the train. It was still repeating itself in his mind when the train pulled into Tuskegee. It followed him to the very door of his room.

Carver was very curious about this school to which he had come, and he wasted no time getting acquainted with it.

"Don't expect too much of us," Washington said to him before he started out to tour the grounds. "We are very poor, you know—poor in everything but spirit. We have plenty of that. Most of our students work their way through. Some of them take seven and eight years to do it. Many work ten hours a day and go to class a couple of hours at night."

Carver understood very well what that meant. He had worked his way through school, too.

"I like the idea of having everybody learn some trade," he thought as he walked along. He had always dreamed about a school where he would teach the things he knew how to do with his hands. He wasn't going to do that here, but he liked being part of such a school anyway.

He looked into the shops where the different trades were taught. He watched students building a wagon, making harness, fashioning saddles and shoes, mattresses and brooms. In a basement he saw girls doing laundry work. His fingers itched to pick up an iron and show them exactly how a collar should be turned.

But the thing he was most interested in, naturally, was the hilltop where the agricultural building was to go up. Washington had told him that a mill owner in Connecticut had given the school $10,000 for the building. The students would start working on it pretty soon.

From the hilltop Carver could see the whole place. He couldn't help sighing as he looked around at the 2,000-acre farm. The land was just the same kind he had seen out of the train window. Much of the top soil was gone. Everywhere he looked he saw shifting sands and gullies. Here and there was a yucca or a cactus. What promise was there in this land?

" 'Big Hungry' is what we call it," one of the students told him.

"It suits the land," Carver answered, thinking,

"I'll have to pioneer the way I did in the desert."

He had a fine title. He was Director and Instructor in Scientific Agriculture and Dairy Science. But the department itself was not much more than a name.

The dairy was a churn under a tree. The agricultural building was just on paper. There was no laboratory, no equipment. To work the sad looking land there was one yoke of oxen. A few sheep and cows made up the stock. There were, indeed, some thirty lean razorback hogs in the pine woods. But Carver could see that no amount of feeding would turn those swift-running creatures into prize animals. As for poultry, all he could see were the buzzards that flapped their great wings around the kitchen waste.

With a sigh he remembered the rich acres of the Iowa Agricultural Experiment Station. A vision of the stately barns and silos and powerful farm machinery came before him. He saw again the sleek cattle, the blue-ribbon hogs and sheep, the prize poultry, the orchards, the greenhouses.

He was heartsick. When he got back from his tour of the grounds, the first thing he did was find Washington. There were things he simply must have to work with.

"Well, Carver! Tell me what you think of Tuskegee!" Washington said cheerfully.

"There is a great deal to be done," Carver answered.

"I know there is," Washington agreed. "I know there is. But give us time, Carver. I assure you things will be different in time. Look how far we've got in fifteen years. Why, when the school started, we had to hold classes in a stable and a hen house. Now, as you see, we have a fine brick building."

A look of pride passed over the principal's face as he said "brick building."

"You are from the North, Carver," he went on. "You cannot possibly know what it means to Negroes in the South to have a brick building of their own. A tumble-down cabin is all these students have ever lived in. We made every one of those bricks ourselves. With our own hands we built that building. As for the Department of Agriculture, it's way ahead of where it was. It started out with just an ax and a hoe, and now look at what you've got."

Carver's tongue stuck to the roof of his mouth. He couldn't bring himself to complain. There was something about this principal that made you feel it was a privilege to work with bare hands.

"Your main problem, Carver," Washington went on, "is your students. We've only thirteen for you to begin with."

"Thirteen students in the whole department?" Carver repeated in astonishment. "But there are a thousand here."

"Well, you see, farming is what our people in the South have always done. Farming is something that in their minds is connected with slavery. They come here thinking they want to study Latin and Greek. They think that's education and will make fine gentlemen and ladies of them. We have to teach them that there's dignity in working with their hands. It will be up to you to show your students there is as much dignity in tilling a field as there is in writing a poem."

"I agree with you," Carver said, "fully."

"But I tell you what." Washington said, "If I were you, I'd not call it farming at all—say *agriculture* instead. I think your students will like agriculture a lot better than farming."

Carver laughed. He felt better after talking with Washington—and suddenly it came to him why. He had the answer to the question that had so bothered him on the train.

"I'll begin right where I am," he thought. "I'll do with what I have."

In the days when he needed a laundry tub and didn't have twenty-five cents to pay for it, Carver would take a barrel and saw it off and make a tub. "Surely I haven't grown less resourceful," he thought. "With thirteen young men to help me I ought to be able to make a few of the things we need. Equipment is not all in the laboratory. Some of it should be in the head of the man running the laboratory."

And he took his students out to search the rubbish heaps.

"Boys," he said, "we're not going to whine that we haven't this and haven't that. Let's see how ingenious we can be. Now use your eyes and use your heads."

A few days later a laboratory was in working order —and it hadn't cost a cent. Broken bottles with their necks cut off evenly had turned into beakers. An old ink bottle with a wick made of twisted string stuck through a cork served for a Bunsen burner. A chipped teacup did duty as a mortar to crush things in. Fruit jar lids held chemicals. A flat iron stood ready to pound things to a powder. Pieces of tin with holes of various sizes punched in them had become sifters for grading soil. Reeds turned into tubes to measure and transfer liquids.

There was just one expensive thing in the entire laboratory, and that was the microscope Carver had brought along with him. He had received it as a parting gift from his teachers and friends in Iowa.

The thirteen students were proud. Up to now they hadn't been certain they wanted to study scientific agriculture. But now they were sure. This lean, stoop-shouldered professor with the handle-bar mustache and the soft smile had a way of turning everything into an adventure. The commonest things became wonderful when he talked about them. Plants and animals and even the very stones and earth under your feet became exciting.

"Well, but what's scientific agriculture about anyway?" other students asked the thirteen.

"Oh, it's about soil and plants and animals and human beings. Professor Carver says they all go together. There's the soil. It's got fourteen elements in it that plants feed on, and you've got to have enough of each one for the particular crop you're going to raise. There's the plant that grows on the soil. It's got to give the animal or human being that eats it 100 percent nourishment at the least possible cost. Scientific farming is doing that without wearing out the soil."

This was certainly different from farming as they knew it. Everybody on the campus buzzed about the new professor.

Even students who weren't studying scientific agriculture got interested. One by one and two by two they joined Carver's classes. By the time the year ended, the thirteen students in the Department of Agriculture had grown to seventy-six, and there were thirty-six in the Dairy.

Carver found himself busier and busier. Besides the classwork there were a million practical things to plan and direct and oversee. There were the animals to care for, and the dairy work to do, fences to fix, landscaping to work out. Every day some new problem would come up. "That's in your department," Washington would say. And it would be up to Carver and his students to take care of it. The Department of Scientific Agriculture was small, but it was the busiest on the campus.

Yet all the time Carver was thinking about being still busier. He went to see Washington.

"It's all very fine to train students in scientific agriculture," he began. "And it's very fine to have them go back to the place they came from and teach others—and they will. But this process is too slow. We can't reach enough farmers that way."

"What do you suggest?" Washington asked.

"An Agricultural Experiment Station. Right here at Tuskegee. We must show the farmers round about us by example what can be done on this worn-out soil."

"What exactly have you in mind?"

"I am not sure yet," Carver answered. "But one thing I do know: growing nothing but cotton ruins the land and wastes the lives of the people. We must show the farmers that it pays to raise other things. We have to experiment with this crop and with that one till we find a way out."

Washington thought for a moment. Then he said, "You draw up a plan, Carver, and I'll start pushing. I think Alabama will agree to an Experiment Station for the colored race—half the people of this state are colored. If you can find a way out. . . ."

"I am full of hope," Carver replied. "I have examined the soil, and though it looks hopeless, I know it can be redeemed. I think we can do things with it."

"Any Farmer Can Do the Same Thing."

14

"THERE'S NO USE TRYING TO MAKE A FARM HERE, PROfessor," the students complained when Carver told them about the Experiment Station. "We've already tried it, and we couldn't make it pay. Ask Mr. Washington. He'll tell you, sir. We lost $16.50 on an acre."

"Never mind what you did before. We are going to doctor the soil."

The boys thought it would take a lot of doctoring. They knew this soil—clay underneath and sandy on top, worn out and washed out. Some of the gullies were actually valleys. One was twenty-five feet deep —you could drop a wagon and team of horses into it and they'd be hidden.

"This soil," Carver declared, "is not so bad as it looks. It will respond to treatment. I believe it is one of the easiest soils to doctor in the entire country. The trouble is that nobody is showing the farmers how to do it. That's our job. Now plow deep. We want twenty acres to experiment on."

The State Legislature had voted $1,500 to be used for an Agricultural Experiment Station for the colored race. It wasn't nearly enough to cover everything—certainly not fertilizer.

"Suppose I write and ask a fertilizer company to *give* us some," Washington suggested. "They just might."

The fertilizer company answered politely. It was all in favor of making experiments on Southern soils. "But we are convinced," the company wrote, "that there is only one colored man capable of doing the experiments you have in mind, and he, unfortunately, is in Iowa."

"We have him right here!" Washington wrote back in a hurry.

A shipment of several hundred pounds of fertilizer

arrived. Carver was grateful, but at the same time he felt uncomfortable about using it.

"We are doing something unfair," he told the students. "Actually we ought to work under the same conditions as the farmers around us. They can't pay for commercial fertilizer; so we shouldn't use it either."

"We could use manure," one of the boys proposed.

"No. The farmers around here don't keep stock; so they have no manure. We have to find some other way of doctoring the soil."

Carver racked his brain what to do. Then early one morning he got an idea.

He was always up and in the woods at four o'clock in the morning to gather specimens and get close to the Creator. On his way home he generally passed the trash heaps, where very often he would pick up something for the laboratory. This morning, happening to look up to the top of the pile, he saw a large plant of some sort growing up on top. What was it?

He climbed up to see. The plant was a magnificent pumpkin vine growing right out of what looked to be a mass of tin cans. It was the very best pumpkin vine Carver had ever seen. It had seven runners nearly forty feet long, and each of them was loaded with big, healthy pumpkins.

When later in the day Carver met his students, he had a broad grin on his face.

"Boys," he said, "I have the answer to our problem." And he took them out on the dump.

"A pumpkin seed," he said, "somehow found its way into this waste. And look what happened. Is it not proof that rotted leaves and grass and rags and paper make very good fertilizer? We will level this trash pile down and rake it over and plant it with cantaloupe and watermelon and onions and potatoes. And at the same time we'll start a compost pile to serve our other fields."

He had the boys build a pen. Anything that would rot quickly was thrown into the pen. Leaves went in and paper and rags and grass—even street sweepings. On top of everything he had the boys throw rich earth from the woods and muck from the swamps. When the whole was well rotted, the students spread it over their fields.

"Now we are not taking an unfair advantage," Carver said. "Any farmer can do the same thing."

Any farmer could also plant the pea family.

"The pea family," Carver explained to the boys, "is the magician among plants. It can pluck nitrogen right out of the air—which is something no other plant can do. All others take nitrogen, which is their most important food, *out* of the soil. But the pea family puts nitrogen *into* the soil. Now we have to find out which member of the pea family does the best all around job."

So the students planted crimson clover and cowpeas and hairy vetch. They planted peanuts and velvet beans and soybeans. And they watched to see which would come out best.

When the cowpeas won, Carver put out a bulletin explaining why farmers should plant them. They were good food for man and for beast, he wrote. Besides, they would put $25 worth of nitrogen into every acre. At the end Carver gave eighteen different recipes for cooking cowpeas.

But what was the use of a bulletin for people who couldn't read?

Carver went to talk things over with Washington.

"We're putting the fodder too high," he told the principal. "If we want farmers to eat of the fruit of knowledge, we've got to put it within their reach. They can't *read* about what we do. They've got to see it."

"Well, let them come here, then, and see it."

"That's just what I came to talk to you about,"

Carver said. "We've got an Institute here for young men and women. How about an Institute for Farmers?"

Washington didn't understand.

"What I mean is this," Carver explained. "Why can't farmers and their wives come here and get one day of school every month of the year? They are hungry for it."

The principal's eyes shone. "Carver, you go right ahead," he said. "We are here to help the man furthest down."

So the Farmers' Institute started. Every third Tuesday in the month, wagons from the nearby region would arrive. Carver would take the farmers all over the experimental acres so they could see for themselves how the sick soil had come back. On the ground that had been a dump they could see a twenty pound cabbage growing. They could handle onions that were seven inches across. They could see great juicy watermelons and cantaloupes. They could dig up a potato plant and see clusters of large, smooth, Irish potatoes.

Carver didn't talk above their heads; he didn't put the fodder too high. He told the farmers in simple language what happens to soil when you plant the same crop year after year. He told them about the washing away of the land.

"We are sinning against the land," he said, "and in return it is punishing us."

He told them about swamp muck and compost. He told them about cowpeas.

And they told him about their problems.

Carver liked the third Tuesday in the month better than any other day. On that day he felt as if he really got to his people.

"Seventy-five farmers are not many out of the millions," he thought. "But seventy-five is better than none. After all, it takes only a little yeast to raise a loaf of bread."

The Man Furthest Down

15

ALL WINTER LONG GEORGE CARVER STAYED RIGHT ON the campus. Very seldom did he even go into the town of Tuskegee. But when summer time came and school closed, he began to roam far afield.

That summer he was looking for plants from which medicines could be made. Often his hunting took him into the swamps among lizards and frogs and snakes and mosquitoes. He didn't mind—a new plant was worth any amount of trouble and discomfort.

One afternoon when he was on a plant hunting trip, Carver had an adventure. Suddenly on the edge of a lonely swamp he came upon a human being. It was an old colored man, and he was doing what to Carver seemed an amazing thing. He was digging up muck. A tall basket stood beside him. He was shoveling muck into the basket.

"Good evening," Carver said. "What are you going to do with that muck?"

"Going to put it on my land," the man answered.

"Why, where did you learn that trick?" Carver asked. "I thought I was the only one that knew it."

"My old master. He did it," the man answered. "Used to send me in the woods rake up oak leaves and go down in the swamp bring up muck. Put it all in the field. Make things grow."

Carver looked at the wise old farmer with delight. "Finest fertilizer there is," the professor said. "Every idle moment should be used gathering it up the way you are doing. . . . I'd like to see your land," he added. He introduced himself. "I teach the boys at Tuskegee how to farm."

The old man looked at him with solemn respect.

"My name's Baker, Henry Baker," he said. "If you want to see my land, my place is just over yonder.

You can see the roof from here if you know where to look."

He lifted the heavy basket, and together they trudged through the swamp.

Carver was expecting to see the usual rickety, saddle-back cabin. But no. To his surprise the roof did not cave in in the middle. The chimney was not propped up by sticks. The door did not hang askew. The spaces between the boards were neatly packed with clay. The pigsty stood way off under a tree instead of right by the door.

Carver could not feast his eyes enough on this neat little cabin. Henry Baker had his own well. He had a cow. Behind the house was a little patch of green corn. In the hollow, sugar cane was growing.

An old woman with a yellow bandanna around her head came out of the cabin to greet them.

"Professor Carver been hunting herbs, Sally," the old man explained.

Carver opened his specimen box to show her the herbs he had gathered.

"Land sakes!" Sally Baker exclaimed. "Is they good for the pellagra? Lots of folks round here got the pellagra bad." Then without waiting for an answer, she turned toward the house. "I got the corn bread in the oven," she said. "You all can set down in just another minute."

The two men went to look at the cotton.

"It's better than most I've seen around here," Carver said. "Still there are not enough bolls on it. I am breeding some new kinds that will give you more to the acre than you are getting now. But you've got too much land in cotton. It's not good for the land to grow just one thing. You want to plant some cow-peas. Plant some sweet potatoes, too—and peanuts."

In the clean, one-room cabin they sat down to a supper of side meat, corn bread and molasses.

"The food of the South," Carver thought. "In two million cabins families are sitting down to this same food that leaves them weak and without health. No vegetables, no proteins. Fat of pork instead of real meat. No eggs. No wonder there's so much pellagra in the South."

"You're from the North, Professor?" Sally Baker asked politely. "Our preacher, he from the North. He say the folks up there don't live poor like us down here."

"Well, to tell you the truth, Mrs. Baker, the home I like best to remember is a one-room cabin in Missouri," Carver answered.

And he told them about Uncle Mose and Aunt Sue and all that they did and had. He told them about the fruits and the nuts and the vegetables, the butter and the cheese and the eggs, the cured meats and the preserves. "There was nothing wasted on their farm," he said. "There was plenty for all. They 'lived at home.' "

Sally and Henry Baker sat there drinking in every word.

"You could make your place like that," Carver said. "You could 'live at home,' too. Why, here in the South almost anything will grow. You've got a long growing season, plenty of rain. You could have fresh vegetables the year around. You should have a garden, Mr. Baker. I'll bring you some seeds."

He nodded towards the open door. "I see you've got a lot of wild plum around. But you could raise peaches and pears and cherries and persimmons. You could have berry bushes and walnuts and pecans. And chickens—you must have chickens. I'll bring you a coop and show you how to set hens so you'll have good luck with them."

Afterwards, when Carver was leaving, Henry Baker said, "I want to thank you, Professor, for your kindness. I is just one farmer, and you done took all that time telling me how I should live. But, Professor, I got neighbors that's worse off than what I is. I owns my land. They just rents it. If you tell me when you're going to bring them seeds and that chicken coop, I'll get my neighbors here. And you can tell them all about how it ain't good for the land to grow just one thing all the time—and about 'live at home.' "

"That's a fine idea," Carver said. "I'll come next Saturday. Tell the wives to come, too—I'll have things to show them."

He was very excited about the idea of bringing school right out to the farmers. Between then and Saturday, Carver spent all his time getting ready. He built himself a big wooden box. Then he started to cook. Into his box he put jars of jam he had made out of wild plums and sealed with white of egg. He put in jars of cowpeas cooked in different ways. He put in cured meat and scrapple and liver puddings. There were vegetables of all kinds. And there were dozens of packets of seeds which Professor Wilson, who was now United States Secretary of Agriculture, had sent him.

Twenty farmers and their wives had gathered in the Baker cabin. They filled the little room to overflowing.

"Now you all just have to set on the floor," Henry Baker said, "while Professor Carver tells you about 'live at home.' "

And Carver told them. He talked about the land and about cotton and about cowpeas. He showed them the jars of food he had brought and let them taste everything. He showed them his prize vegetables that had grown on a dump. Before their astonished eyes he cut open a juicy tomato and ate it. They had never seen anybody eat a tomato before. Always they had been told tomatoes were poison.

Carver showed them how to set a hen so all the chicks would hatch. He told them about curing meat so it would keep through the heat of summer. He told them how to make scrapple and liver pudding.

" 'Live at home,' " Carver said. "Don't buy everything you need at the plantation owner's store. Grow your own food. A garden is the best doctor there is."

Then he gave each man some garden seeds. Last of all he passed out flower seeds.

"Don't forget the dooryard," he said. "A flower is God's silent messenger. It's the sweetest thing he ever made and forgot to put a soul into."

After that day a week seldom passed that Carver didn't drive out to talk to the farmers in one part of Macon County or another. On Friday afternoons when school was over, out would come the big wooden box. The mule would be hitched up, and Carver would be off to the far places.

But it was slow work getting things across to the man furthest down.

"So few of the farmers own their own land," Carver thought. "That's why. Many more would be like Baker if they owned their farms."

And he started urging farmers to save so they could buy some land.

"Put away five cents every working day," he would say. "At the end of a year you will have $15.50. That's enough to buy three acres of land and fifty cents left over."

It pained him to see the weather-beaten, saddle-back cabins. There was so little comfort, so little beauty in and around them. He had given the farmers flower seeds. Here and there you could now see a spot of color by a cabin. But a few flowers couldn't take away the drabness. What could he do to improve these ugly shacks which people had no money to rebuild?

Night after night Carver went to bed thinking about it. In the morning before the sun was up he would be in the woods. While he gathered plant specimens, he would seek the answer to his problem. He felt very close to God in the woods at dawn. "If I only open my eyes and my mind wide enough, I will understand what God means for me to do," he thought.

One morning coming out of the woods he paused to look at the rolling country. The sun had just come up, and it lighted up a great bank of clay. Carver's eye was caught as never before by the rich colors of the clay—red and yellow and tan and cream and pure white. What was the purpose of these bright clays? Could he make something out of them to bring cheer to the drab little cabins?

He took some handfuls of white clay to the laboratory. By night he had the answer.

It was so simple that he wondered afterwards why no one had ever thought of it. The clay could be made to yield an excellent whitewash. All you had to do was get the sand out and dissolve the clay in water.

Now at least the interior of the shacks could become clean and cheerful. A coat of whitewash would brighten the ugliest walls. Cellar and stable and barn, hen house and pigsty could all be freshened up. And it wouldn't cost the farmers a cent.

God directing him, he had found out the meaning of white clay, and now it was just a step to learn the meaning of the other clays. In the weeks that followed, Carver got a yellow wash from the yellow clay. He made blueing from rotten sweet potatoes, added it to the yellow and got green. In all, twenty-seven different color washes came out of the clay before Carver was through with it.

Up to this time he had always thought of his laboratory as a place to analyze things and find out what they were made of. Now he began to think of the laboratory in a new way. It was a workshop. It was a place for making things.

God directing him, what more would he be able to make for the man furthest down?

"Plant Peanuts!"

16

LONG AGO WHEN HE WAS A CHILD WITH AUNT SUE, George Carver had planted flowers close together to see if they would mix. Later on he had learned that bees do the mixing by carrying pollen from flower to flower. When he found that he himself could do the work of bees, a new world had opened for him.

Mostly he worked with flowers that spring from bulbs. That was because in those days he was always on the move and could carry the bulbs from place to place in his pocket. Amaryllis was his pet. Everywhere he went, the rosy amaryllis went with him. He developed many varieties. One was a pure white. One was ten inches across.

In Iowa he went from flowers to fruit, creating new varieties of apples, pears, plums. By the time he left for the South, he was one of the best plant breeders in the world.

What would he breed at Tuskegee?

"No matter what I do," Carver said to himself, "a large part of the farmers' crop will be cotton. At least I can give them a good variety to grow. They don't have to keep on planting cotton that bears just two bolls on a stalk."

So he planted and cross-bred cotton. Year after year he worked to develop kinds that would have more and bigger bolls on each plant. By 1909 he had created four new varieties. One had bolls of enormous size—275 of them on a single bush. The yield was nearly a bale and a quarter an acre.

The farmers of Macon County couldn't believe their ears when they heard about that cotton. How was it possible? Here they had been planting cotton all their lives and all they could raise was a third of a bale on an acre. And this man Carver had never even seen cotton growing till he came to Tuskegee.

The whole county, white folk and black, talked about the cotton up at Tuskegee.

The thing that puzzled the white planters most was that a Negro had raised it. How could any black man have brains enough to get a bale and a quarter of cotton from an acre of land? Was it really true that he was a full-blooded Negro? Maybe he had some white blood in him. They came up to see.

People from abroad didn't worry their heads about such nonsense. They didn't share the Southern white man's feelings about the Negro. An important visitor from Germany got so excited about the cotton that he asked for three graduates from Tuskegee to go to the West Coast of Africa and show the people in the German colonies how to grow cotton. A visitor from Australia carried away seeds so he could introduce the cotton into his own country.

Carver took it in his stride. He had been doing this sort of thing all his life. What was so wonderful about it? He had done with cotton no more than he had done with amaryllis.

But Washington was proud. He was the leader of his race. Anything a Negro did—good or bad—was important to him. Negroes were always on trial. If a Negro did something bad, people said it was because he was a Negro. If he did something good, they said he must have white blood in him. But just the same what he had done reflected honor on the whole race. And George Washington Carver had done something to serve every cotton farmer, white as well as black.

"People are making too much fuss about this cotton," Carver told Washington. "I would be better pleased if I could get the farmers to plant some crop besides cotton."

"You are doing it," the principal said. "A lot of our people are raising vegetables now. I see vegetable gardens and chickens all over Macon County. Our people are living better. They are eating better. There is less sickness."

"Well, yes, I know that," Carver said. "The other day I walked in on a farm family when they weren't expecting me. They were just sitting down to supper, and, of course, they asked me to eat with them. I remember when that family used to eat nothing but the three M's—meat, meal, and molasses. Now they 'live at home.' We had ham that was raised on the place, home-made butter, eggs, two kinds of canned fruit, and biscuits with syrup. The flour had been bought with egg money."

"A right good supper."

"It was. But 'living at home' doesn't take much land. And as long as most of it stays in cotton, the South will remain poor."

They were both thoughtful a moment. Then Washington said, "In a way, you can't blame the Negro farmers. Most of them don't own their land—they *have* to plant what the plantation owner says."

"That's very true," Carver agreed. "And look how the thing works out. If the farmers have a good crop, the price of cotton goes down and they don't make any money. If the weather is bad, they lose everything. . . . I am looking for some native plant they can grow and sell instead of cotton."

"You have been working with the sweet potato, I know."

"The sweet potato has a lot of possibilities," Carver answered. "When we first started growing it, we got forty bushels from an acre. Now the forty bushels have jumped to 266. We can get more bushels of sweet potatoes out of an acre of land than we can of any other crop. With care we can raise two crops a year. They're easy to grow. And the wonderful part of it is that sweet potatoes do less harm to the soil than anything else. They get almost all their nourishment from the air."

"Then you think the answer to the cotton problem is sweet potatoes?"

"I don't know. Sweet potatoes don't keep well," said Carver. "But one thing is sure—help must come from somewhere, and right quick. Pretty soon the cotton farmer is going to have a worse enemy than weather. The Mexican boll weevil is heading this way. It was already in Texas when I came here. Now it is eating its way through Louisiana and Mississippi. Once it gets to Alabama, there will be mighty little cotton left for our farmers. They *must* plant something else instead."

Carver was spending a great deal of time in his laboratory now. If the farmers were going to raise sweet potatoes, he must find ways of using them. There wasn't much of a market for sweet potatoes—they spoiled too easily.

So in his laboratory the professor dried sweet potatoes and ground them and made a coffee substitute out of them. He peeled and grated them and out of their milky juice made starch. He boiled the water that settled on top and made a syrup.

Then he went out and taught the farmers. "Lay the sweet potatoes out in the sun and dry them—or dry them on the back of your stoves." He showed the wives how to make sweet potato starch and coffee and syrup.

And he told the farmers about the boll weevil.

"That little black bug," he said, "is coming, and you had better get ready. If you go on planting only cotton, you will be in trouble deep. The boll weevil will eat you out of house and home. Nothing will stop that little bug. Plant enough sweet potatoes so you can sell some. Plant cowpeas. Plant peanuts. They will be your cash crop."

Peanuts? The farmers opened their eyes wide at that one. A few families grew a few peanut vines. But that was only on account of the children. The children loved goobers. But could goobers be a farm crop?

Carver had wondered about that himself once. Lately he had stopped wondering. He had come to believe that the answer he had so long looked for lay in sweet potatoes and peanuts—in those two together. Together they could be the life-savers of the South. They could even lick the boll weevil.

Peanuts were not a new idea with him. He had started planting them 'way back in 1896. But that was on account of the nitrogen they put back into the soil. At that time he hadn't known much about the nuts themselves. Since then he had taken the peanut into the laboratory and been amazed by what he found. The peanut was an almost magical food.

It was chock full of nourishment. A pound of peanuts contained more protein than a pound of sirloin steak. It contained as much carbohydrates as a pound of potatoes. And on top of all that it had one-third as much fat as a pound of butter.

"Plant sweet potatoes, plant peanuts," Carver told the farmers.

He published a bulletin giving directions for growing peanuts. At the end he gave 105 peanut recipes.

One day he said to Washington: "Ask some of your friends to lunch. The Senior girls will cook it. Everything will be made of peanuts."

Ten people sat down to table. The girls served a five course meal.

First came soup, then mock chicken with peanuts creamed as a vegetable and peanut bread. After that there was a salad. After the salad came ice cream and cookies. Last of all coffee and candy were served. Everything was made from peanuts and nothing tasted the same. One guest after another declared, "I have never eaten a tastier or more satisfying lunch."

"Plant peanuts," Carver told the farmers.

Some of the Negro farmers listened. The peanut

was a curious plant, but they had grown up with it and understood its ways. Even their ancestors in Africa had known the peanut. It had traveled from Peru to Spain, from Spain to Africa, from Africa back with the slaves. "Goober" was one of the few African words in the English language.

The Negro farmers listened. Peanuts were easy to raise. Peanuts didn't mind a drought. When there was no rain, they just curled up and waited for it. Then when rain came, the plants raced right ahead. The flowers matured and withered. The stems grew long and bent towards the ground. The pods dug themselves into the earth. In the earth, in the dark, they ripened like potatoes.

Some of the white farmers listened to Carver, too. The man who had raised nearly a bale and a quarter of cotton on an acre was worth listening to. Here and there acres of peanuts began to take the place of cotton.

One day a woman came to Carver. She was a widow, managing a big farm, she said. She had read his bulletin and followed his advice—she had put in a great crop of peanuts. When they were ripe, she had harvested and dried them according to his directions. Then she had taken them to market. And nobody had wanted to buy her peanuts!

"What am I to do now?" she asked. "Here I have gone and done just what you said. I have raised peanuts and now they are on my hands. I can't sell them."

Carver was greatly disturbed. He saw now that he hadn't thought the problem all the way through. Growing peanuts and sweet potatoes instead of cotton was only half the answer. A market was the other half.

He was sure he hadn't made a mistake about peanuts. They were one of God's greatest gifts. People just didn't know it. They thought of peanuts as "monkey food"—something to take with you when you went to the zoo. They thought peanuts were for circuses and carnivals, a treat for the children, that's all.

For such things there were enough peanuts being imported from abroad. What was to be done with the extra ones?

"I have to find ways of using peanuts so there will be a market for them," Carver told the woman.

And he shut himself up in his laboratory to try.

God's Little Workshop

ALL HIS LIFE GEORGE CARVER HAD GOT UP AT FOUR o'clock in the morning. Now he began to get up at three. He would go first to the woods and then straight to his laboratory—God's Little Workshop everyone called it. There he would lock himself in with his peanuts. He didn't want anyone to bother him while he worked. He didn't want anyone to ask him questions or distract him just by being there.

For weeks already he had worked to break up the

peanut. Now it was done. In the jars and bottles and test tubes around him were all the different parts. He knew exactly what the peanut was made of now. Water, fats, oils, gums, resins, sugars, starches, pectoses, pentosans, amino acids—he could use any or all of them.

He put on his big laboratory apron and a pair of black sleeves to protect his sweater. He drew a rack of test tubes towards him. For a moment he stood surveying the different parts of the peanut trying to make up his mind where to begin.

Generally he planned his experiments the night before and had everything laid out to work with. But today he wasn't quite sure what he would do. He might start one thing and then change to something else—he would keep his spirit free to follow any lead.

"Tell me, Great Creator, why did you make the peanut?"

Very often this thought passed through the professor's head. For he believed firmly that everything had been made for a purpose. Now he said the words aloud. And in the silence of the lonely room it seemed to him that he heard a voice answering.

"I have given you three laws—compatibility, temperature, and pressure. All you have to do is take the different parts of the peanut and put them together.

Observe the laws. And I will show you why I made the peanut."

A hundred experiments flashed through the professor's mind. He would put the parts of the peanut together again—but in different ways. He would try combining this part with that under different conditions. He would use more heat or less, use more pressure or less.

Professor Carver lit his Bunsen burner. He took up a clean test tube. With God directing him, what would come from his hands?

"What's that man Carver doing in there?" the teachers asked one another. The school had grown, and now there were eighty-six teachers at Tuskegee "Why does he get up at such an unearthly hour? Why does he lock the door and not let anybody in?"

They thought him queer. He was so different from other people. He was always doing things they couldn't understand—like eating weeds and saying they were good food. Imagine putting chick weed in your salad! Imagine eating clover tops and pepper grass, purslane and shepherd's purse!

With him it was always work, work, work. Even his play was work—he would stay in his rooms and paint or make lace. And nobody could get in to clean his place. He wouldn't let anybody scrub his floors. Insisted on doing it himself. Said he had made the soap himself and wanted to see how it worked. It was so undignified to act like that!

They didn't know that Carver did his own scrubbing because he was afraid an ignorant person might throw away some very important plant specimen—a rare fungus perhaps. But they did know that his rooms were so cluttered up with things there was no place to sit down. Papers and books were piled high on every chair. Every inch of space near the windows was taken up by plants. Amaryllis. He said he was developing one that would bloom twice a year.

His office was worse than his rooms. Every time he came back from outdoors he brought some new thing he had picked up somewhere. He had the tooth of a mastodon and the skeleton of a prehistoric lizard. One day he came lugging a great heavy piece of metal, said it was a meteorite. "This is one of the 'stars' that fell on Alabama," he said. Limbs of trees, moss, snake skins, feathers—you could find any crazy thing in his office. And he encouraged his students and the children around Tuskegee to bring things in. He helped them stuff their dead birds and animals.

He looked so shabby. He sewed on his own buttons and kept his clothes mended, but he never bought a new suit—always it was a second-hand one. If you gave him a tie, he wouldn't wear it. He liked the ones he dyed himself better. "There goes the great Professor Carver. He looks like a ragamuffin." Someone was always saying that.

And he had no sense about money. He gave away most of his salary, helping this student and that. When he had a chance to get rich, what did he do? Turned it down.

That blue color of his. He had got a wonderful blue pigment out of red clay, a rare color that could be used in oil paints and water colors, a blue that wouldn't fade. He had displayed it along with his color washes at a fair and someone from a great Northern paint company had spotted it. The company sent a man to Tuskegee to talk to Carver about it.

"Your blue is seventy times bluer than blue!" the company's representative said enthusiastically.

"Yes, it is very beautiful," Carver answered. "The ancient Egyptians loved this blue so much they used to decorate their tombs with it."

"We would like to have you help us put it on the market," the paint company's man said.

"No, no, no!" Carver had cried. "I am not here to

go into business or to help some rich Northern firm get richer. I am here to help the man furthest down. I don't want my name used now or ever."

They couldn't understand him. Maybe if he had a wife she would put some money sense into him.

"Why don't you get married?" the teachers asked him sometimes.

"I haven't the time," Carver would answer.

But he had time to send flower seeds to anyone who asked for them. He had time to stop in and tell someone what disease her roses had and what to do for them. He had time to travel out to the little Tuskegees his students were setting up in the places from which they had come. He had time to hold a Bible class. He had time to talk to children.

No, most of the teachers couldn't understand Professor Carver. He was too different.

But Washington understood. Washington felt very close to Carver. They were two very different men, and sometimes they disagreed. But there was nobody at Tuskegee whom the principal respected more.

Yet even Washington couldn't understand the professor's passion for the laboratory. Recently Carver had said he would have to leave Tuskegee if he couldn't spend all his time experimenting. Washington had given in—he could not dream of letting Carver go away. They had compromised; Professor Carver would just teach a couple of classes at night.

In God's Little Workshop, George Carver was working with the peanut. He had not yet learned all the reasons why God had made it. But every day or two a new bottle or jar or box containing a new wonder joined the collection on the shelves.

Here were foods of all kinds—meal, instant coffee, chili sauce, mixed pickles, a dozen different drinks.

Here were salve, bleach, ink, rubbing oil, shampoo, shaving cream, axle grease, metal polish.

Here were linoleum, paper, plastics, wood filler, washing powder, synthetic rubber.

And here was peanut milk. Cream would rise upon it as on cow's milk. You could take the cream off and make it into butter. You could make it into cheese.

And still George Carver went on exploring the peanut. It was magical. He had passed the hundred mark, had passed the two hundred mark. Surely amongst these many products there must be some that would create a market for the peanut. Surely someone would come along and say, "I will build a factory and manufacture shaving cream." Or metal polish. Or some other product.

But at times it seemed almost as if Professor Carver had forgotten the reason why he started working on the peanut. What he was doing in itself fascinated him. He was discovering, creating. All his life he had explored the mineral, vegetable, and animal kingdoms. Now he had flung wide the door of the fourth, the synthetic kingdom. To him it seemed the most wonderful kingdom of all.

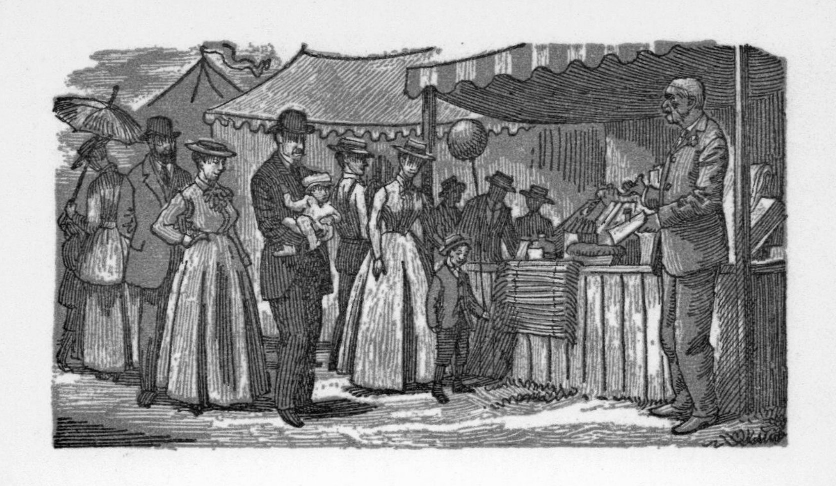

Blazing the Way

18

FROM THE TIME HE UNLOCKED THE PEANUT'S SECRETS, Professor Carver's head was filled with dreams. Often there was a far-off look on his face as if he saw something no one else could see. And it was true. He had a vision of a new South. It was a South prosperous because in it farms and factories went together.

All through Alabama now people were in despair about the boll weevil. They said it had turned the

South into a poorhouse. But Carver told them they were wrong.

"The South is not really poor," he said. "It has more natural advantages than almost any other part of the world. It has a wonderful climate. It has mineral wealth. It has valuable native plants. It has plenty of people to do the work. It could be the richest and most prosperous part of America if it weren't for King Cotton. He it is that keeps the South poor. He kept it poor even before the boll weevil came."

Carver himself had stopped worrying about the boll weevil. In fact, he had come to regard the little black bug as a blessing in disguise. The boll weevil was doing more to turn people from raising cotton than all his talking had done. He had begun to think that God had sent it on purpose—to bring into being that new South of which he dreamed.

The vision filled his mind's eye. People had always thought of farms as growing food for human beings and animals to eat. He saw farms growing food as raw materials for industry. He saw a South in which farmers never had to worry about a market. Factories would take over and transform the extra food they raised. Factories would use even the parts of plants that couldn't be eaten. There was so much waste in stalks and stems and husks and shells! And all of them could be made into useful and beautiful things.

Here was sawdust, for instance.

He took it into God's Little Workshop. He added something to make it stick together, put in color to give it beauty, polished it up. And there were shining slabs of synthetic marble. It was strong, weatherproof, easy to make, cheap.

From peanut shells, from banana stems, from pine cones, wistaria, cotton, pecan shells, he made wall board.

From yucca and peanut skins he made paper fine as linen. It was so strong you could use it for cloth.

He turned cotton stalks into paper and rope and fiber rugs.

He made rugs and rope and paper from okra stems.

He leaped from one task to another.

"Tell us, Professor," people asked in amazement, "how do you create all these wonderful things? Explain it to us."

"There is nothing I can explain," he answered. "I am simply an instrument in God's hands. The thing I am to do always comes to me. I do not have to grope. There comes suddenly the inspiration to create something. I reach out my hand and there it is. The thing is done. And it is right."

In 1915 Theodore Roosevelt came to Tuskegee. Booker T. Washington had died, and many famous men and women came to pay tribute to the great leader of the Negro people. After the ceremonies were over, Roosevelt came to Carver to say good-bye. Arm in arm they walked to the station.

"There *is* no more important work than what you are doing," Roosevelt said.

Many a time in the woods at dawn George Carver had asked God, "What is the plan for me?" He didn't ask it nowadays. The plan was clear—he had been appointed to blaze the path into the new synthetic world.

In 1917 the United States went to war with Germany. All of America's dyes had come from the enemy's country, and now no more were to be had.

George Carver made dyes. Out of twenty-eight different plants he squeezed 536 different dyes. They could be used to stain leather, cotton, wool, silk, linen.

The head of a great dyestuffs firm wrote to Carver. The firm would equip a laboratory for him if he would take charge of it. He could name his own salary. They sent him a check to fill in with any figure he chose.

Sorry. He couldn't leave Tuskegee. Glad to have given them something to work on.

No. He couldn't leave Tuskegee. Now that Booker T. Washington was dead, his people looked to Carver as their leader. If he should go, he would be lost to his people.

Food shortages came. Again Carver turned to the sweet potato.

He made egg yolk and tapioca and breakfast food. He made syrup and vinegar and alcohol.

He made sweet potato flour.

The United States Government heard about it. It had tried all sorts of substitutes for wheat flour to make bread. None was fit to make such bread as Americans were used to. Let this man Carver from Tuskegee come to Washington and demonstrate his sweet potato flour.

Carver went to Washington. He attended a meeting of Army bakers and experts.

"If you will permit me, I will bake you some bread," he said.

The bread came out of the oven brown and crusty and sweet-smelling. He passed pieces around to the experts.

"It is delicious," they exclaimed. "This is the best substitute for wheat flour we have seen."

Carver went back to God's Little Workshop. There

were so many things he wanted to create. He had dozens of ideas, hundreds of ideas.

Products—one more amazing than the next—poured from the laboratory.

"But how are these things to be put on the market?" people asked him.

"I don't know," he answered. "That's not my job."

His job was to blaze the way. Let others pick up where he left off. No, he didn't want to go into business. No, no, he didn't want to be paid! His advice and information were free. "God does not charge us for his wonders. If I charge for anything, I will lose my power," he declared—and returned the checks.

Thomas Edison sent his right hand man to Tuskegee. He talked with Carver, went back and reported to his chief. "That man Carver is worth his weight in gold."

Edison offered the professor a job in his laboratory. The salary would be in six figures.

Was it a hundred thousand dollars or half a million? Carver wouldn't say. He wasn't interested in money.

A great rubber company offered him a position.

No, thank you. He couldn't accept. "I have spent twenty years helping the Negro farmer. If I were to go, my work would not be known as mine. My race would get no credit. I want it to have the credit of whatever I may do."

Washington had given his life for his people. Could he do less?

Peanut Men Get Together

19

IT TAKES COURAGE TO BREAK THE HABIT OF YEARS, AND cotton was an old, old habit. But what with the boll weevil on the one hand and Professor Carver on the other, the peanut was taking hold. By 1919 it had really become a crop.

Who would ever have thought anyone would be grateful to the boll weevil? But there it was. In the public square of Enterprise, Alabama, a monument had been put up to the little black bug.

"In profound appreciation of the boll weevil and what it has done. As the herald of prosperity, this monument was erected by the citizens of Enterprise, Coffee County, Alabama." That's how the inscription read.

It was clear to everyone who saw the fine peanut shelling plant in Enterprise why the monument had been erected. In Coffee County the boll weevil had pushed King Cotton from his throne. King Peanut ruled instead. Every cotton farmer in the county had been so down and out in 1915 that nobody could pay his bills. After four years of raising peanuts, Coffee County was the most prosperous in Alabama.

Yes, peanuts were definitely moving up. They were a crop. In 1919, when Enterprise put up the monument, about half the peanuts consumed in the United States were grown at home. The peanut industry was worth 80 million dollars. That was a lot, but it was nothing to what the industry could be worth. It was an infant as yet. Could anything be done to make it grow faster?

The Southern peanut men got together. They were making money; but who doesn't want to make more? They organized the United Peanut Associations of America and started thinking what they could do to make people use more peanuts.

"We've got to advertise," they decided.

"Right," said one of the peanut men. "But first we ought to educate the public. People don't know anything about peanuts. Some folks think they grow on bushes. Some are scared they'll get a disease from eating peanuts."

Everybody agreed that educating the public was a good idea.

"And it wouldn't be a bad one," the peanut man went on, "if we educated ourselves a little first. There's an old colored man by the name of Carver down at the Tuskegee Institute. I went to see him and spent two very interesting hours with him in his laboratory. This old man has produced a peanut milk. He's made a lot of other things from peanuts besides. And I think we ought to have him come to a meeting and describe to us the things he's made."

Have an old colored man come and tell them about their business? Ridiculous!

That was the opinion of a good many. But more thought otherwise. Peanut milk! They'd like to see that. It was finally agreed that at their September meeting in Montgomery, Carver might come and show them what he had done with the peanut.

Professor Carver had been showing his products at county fairs for a good many years. But he had never wanted to have anything to do with the business end of the things he made. So businessmen didn't know him. Even these men who were making—or trying to make—a fortune out of peanuts had never heard his name. They didn't know it was Carver who had started peanut growing in the South and that they owed their prosperity to him. To them he was "an old colored man down at Tuskegee."

George Carver had long ago found out that being a Negro in the South was a much harder thing than being a Negro in the North.

"Be careful," Washington had warned him when he first came to Tuskegee. "Don't do anything that may displease the white people. The Institute depends on white good will."

And the other teachers had taught him.

"Stand bareheaded when you talk to a white man —any white man. Say 'sir.' When you are in town, walk on the gutter side of the sidewalk so you can be shoved off where you belong. Don't stir out after dark. Don't call any Negro Mr. or Mrs. or Miss— that's too much honor for us."

Carver had learned all the ins and outs of the system and tried to think about it as little as he could. "If I let myself resent these things," he said to himself, "I will have no strength for anything else." And in spite of all the indignities, he went wherever he was called to speak.

For he had come to understand that the South and his people were one and that he could not help his people very much until the whole South changed. Anything he could do to bring into being that land of farms and factories which he saw in his mind's eye he wanted to do.

On the second day of the meeting of the United Peanut Associations, Professor Carver arrived in Montgomery, the capital of Alabama. He had brought with him two heavy cases packed tight with bottles of things to show the peanut men. Carrying a case in either hand, he walked up to the Exchange Hotel.

"What do you want here?" the doorman asked. He stood barring the professor's way.

"I want to see the President of the Peanut Associations, sir," Professor Carver said.

"They're over at the City Hall."

Carver picked up his cases. Through the stifling heat he trudged to City Hall. He blundered from place to place, spoke to this person and that.

"They've been here and gone," a man finally told him.

Once more Carver picked up his cases. He trudged back to the hotel.

"You can't come in here. No niggers allowed!" The doorman stood firmly in his path.

"But they are expecting me!"

It was no use.

"Well, then, will you be kind enough to take a note in? I must get in touch with them."

While a bellhop went up with a note, the professor stood waiting out on the sweltering sidewalk. After a while the boy came back.

"Come along."

He led the professor around a back way and up a freight elevator to the room where the meeting was being held.

Carver was tired and perspiring. He had been tramping around for an hour with two heavy cases and waiting in the hot sun. But no one would have guessed from his manner that he had been through anything. He acted as though indeed these men whom he had come to serve had done him an honor to let him stand before them.

But had they done right to let a Negro come? Watching him open up his cases, the audience was still not sure. Then Carver held up a bottle and began to talk. At once every doubt vanished.

Was it possible? Had all these wonderful things actually come out of the peanut?

Here were leather stains—shading from black to tan to russet. Here were wood stains in glorious colors, among them peacock green and malachite green. Here was Worcestershire sauce. Fruit punch. Instant coffee. Coffee with cream.

And here was that milk they had heard about. And buttermilk . . . cream . . . evaporated milk.

"I thank you for being allowed to contribute in a small way," Carver said when he had finished showing his bottles, "and wish you Godspeed."

The peanut men broke out into loud clapping. They had forgotten that Carver was a member of the Negro race.

A Congressman got up to speak. After the professor's talk, anybody could see, he said, how important peanuts were. But the peanut industry was an infant. It had to be protected. It couldn't grow properly if thirty million pounds of peanuts continued to be brought in from abroad. What the Association had to do was get Congress to put a high tax on foreign peanuts. That would keep them out.

"And when the time comes that this question must be thrashed out before the American Congress, I propose," the Congressman concluded, "to see that Professor Carver is there. Let him instruct them a little about peanuts as he has done here on this occasion."

Everybody clapped. Everybody was excited. Peanuts had a wonderful future! Everybody was going to make a pile of money!

Professor Carver packed up his bottles, picked up his cases, and walked back to the station to catch his train.

Congressmen Listen

20

THE PEANUT MEN HAD GONE HOME CONFIDENT, BUT AS January, 1921 came on, they found themselves getting nervous. In Washington the Ways and Means Committee of Congress was working on the new tariff law. Would the Committee put a high enough tax on foreign peanuts to keep them out of the country?

In the middle of January, Professor Carver got a wire. "Want you in Washington morning of twentieth," the telegram read. "Depending on you to show Ways and Means Committee possibilities of the peanut."

Professor Carver packed up his cases and got on the train.

He had been to Washington before, but he had never been at a Congressional committee meeting. The proceedings were quite a shock to him. He heard people talking in angry tones, shouting at one another, all but calling one another names. Professor Carver felt embarrassed just listening to them.

All morning he sat hearing arguments why there should be a higher tariff on walnuts and pecans. The Committee hadn't got to peanuts yet.

In the afternoon it began again. The hours ran on. The Congressmen looked tired and bored. Only when it got on towards four o'clock did they cheer up. Soon it would be time to go home.

All of a sudden Professor Carver heard his name called. He got up, grasped a case in each hand, and began to move toward the platform.

Everybody stared. Was this old colored fellow going to tell the Ways and Means Committee what it ought to do about peanuts? What could he possibly have to say about peanuts? That he liked to eat them?

"I suppose," one of the Congressmen remarked as Carver passed by, "if you have plenty of peanuts and watermelons, you're perfectly happy?"

Professor Carver didn't reply. He was used to insulting remarks. He kept right on going, pretending he hadn't heard. All the Congressmen looked so bored and anxious to get up and leave that he was wondering what he could say to get them interested from the start.

As he reached the platform, the Chairman called out in an offhand way, "Your time has been cut to ten minutes."

The professor's heart began to race. Ten minutes! How could he possibly show the Committee what was in his cases in that time? It would take him nearly ten minutes just to unpack. Had he come the long way from Tuskegee, sitting up all night in the uncomfortable car provided for Negroes, just to open his cases and shut them up again?

His fingers worked quickly to unpack, and while they did so, his mind found answers for the questions thrown at him. They were foolish questions. The Congressmen were needlessly taking up his precious time.

"Three minutes are gone!" a voice warned.

It was like a bad dream, Professor Carver was sweating from anxiety.

Then his sense of humor came to his rescue. "You took those three minutes," he said, "so I suppose you'll give them back to me."

The Congressmen hadn't expected a sally like that. Some of them laughed. This old colored fellow had his wits about him. This promised to be fun.

Now Carver had got some bottles out and was holding one up.

"This is chocolate covered candy," he said. "You don't know how delicious it is. So I'll taste it for you." And he put one in his mouth.

Everybody was laughing now. Carver felt the ugliness in the air melt away and breathed more easily. Now he could plunge into his subject.

"The sweet potato and the peanut," he began, "are twin brothers and should not be separated. If all other foods were destroyed, these would provide a balanced ration for man."

He held up a bottle of sweet potato syrup that could be used to hold a peanut bar together. "Think of them as twins," he said, "as close as nuts and candy in a bar."

Then one after another he held up meal, breakfast food, flour, the makings of ice cream—all from peanuts.

Already the ten minutes were up, but nobody was

getting up to go. Carver had taken them into the new synthetic world, and they were enthralled.

"I think," Congressman Garner said, "this is very interesting. I think his time should be extended."

Everybody agreed. Everybody looked curiously at Carver. Everybody wondered what marvel the next bottle would contain.

"Peanut skins," Carver said, "are not just something to throw away. They have their uses, too. Here I have a bottle of dye. It is one of thirty dyes I have got out of peanut skins."

"What do you know about the tariff?" Congressman Garner suddenly asked.

"Tariff?" Carver repeated. "This is all the tariff means—to put the other fellow out of business."

There was a roar of laughter. The colored fellow was pretty smart. Say it any way you liked, you couldn't say it better than that!

"Go ahead, brother," the Chairman said when he had stopped laughing. "Your time is unlimited."

Then Professor Carver really went at it. He showed them his peanut milk, on which, everyone could see, cream had risen.

"Good, rich milk," Carver said. "But you can tell the dairymen it's not going to put the cow out of business."

"How does it go in a punch?" someone asked to be funny.

"I will show you some punches," Carver answered and held up one bottle after another.

"And this here is buttermilk. And this—evaporated milk. And here is coffee with cream. Peanuts, I must tell you, make one of the very best cereal coffees."

He held up a bottle of Worcestershire sauce.

"The base of the original Worcestershire sauce was soy beans," he said. "But peanut sauce is just as good.

"And here is cheese. You can make thirty-five pounds of it from a hundred pounds of peanut milk. From the same amount of cow's milk, I would like to point out, you can get only ten pounds of cheese."

"Do you make all these products yourself?" a Congressman asked. There was respect in the lawmaker's voice now.

"Yes, sir. That's what a research laboratory is for," Carver answered.

"Haven't you done something with sweet potatoes?" someone else asked.

"One hundred and seven to date."

"What's that?" Congressman Garner asked. He

thought he hadn't heard right. "Will you repeat it, please?"

"Yes, indeed. I said one hundred and seven, but I have not finished working on them yet. The peanut will beat the sweet potato by far."

Carver had another bottle in his hand. "Here is the latest thing—a face cream, soft and fine as almond cream. And here is one for massaging infants to fatten them. It works better than olive oil."

After the oil came ink, then milk flakes that could be dissolved in water to make milk again. Next came a relish, then mock oysters and a peanut curd which tasted just like meat.

Professor Carver waved a hand towards his cases. "I have two dozen or so others, such as wood dyes and stains. But if my time is up, I'd better stop."

He said this with a twinkle in his eye. Though he had talked for an hour and three quarters instead of ten minutes, he could see that no one was thinking of going.

Congressman Garner spoke up again. "I understood you to say that if all other foods were destroyed, a person could live on sweet potatoes and peanuts?"

"That is correct," Professor Carver answered, "because they contain the necessary vitamins. Together they form a natural food for man and beast. There is everything here to strengthen and nourish and keep the body alive and healthy."

What an amazing fellow this Negro was! With his perfect English and his perfect manners, with his humor and his great knowledge, he was more wonderful than all his bottles put together. And, believe it or not, there was no white blood in him! Anyone could see that.

They were curious about him. What made a man like that?

"Mr. Carver, what school did you attend?" someone asked.

"Iowa State," Professor Carver answered. "Secretary of Agriculture Wilson was my instructor for five years."

"You have rendered the Committee a great service," one of the Congressmen said, speaking for all.

"I think," Congressman Garner added, "he is entitled to the thanks of the Committee." He rose, and to Carver's astonishment all the other Congressmen rose, too, and stood clapping their hands. They stood and clapped for a long time.

Carver bowed. Then he turned and began putting his bottles away.

He could hear the Congressmen talking about the

need for a high tariff. "How high?" Carver wondered. Would it be high enough to put the other fellow out of business? High enough to bring prosperity to all the peanut farmers in the South? High enough to make the cotton farmers switch to peanuts?

It was not till three months later that Professor Carver learned just how successful his trip to Washington had been. The peanut men sent him a marked copy of *The Peanut World,* and in it a whole page was devoted to thanking him. The peanut men called him an "incomparable genius." They said he was "a miracle worker." And they considered their tribute "small in comparison to what he has done for all of us."

Professor Carver Is "Discovered"

21

BY THE TIME THE PEANUT MEN "DISCOVERED" GEORGE Carver, he had been at Tuskegee for a quarter of a century. He had spent it all in hard work, and he asked only to go on working. But it wasn't so easy to shut himself up in God's Little Workshop any more. New groups and individuals were always "discovering" him. They called on him to speak, to lecture, to exhibit.

He traveled here, and he traveled there. Sometimes

for weeks he would ride all day in the uncomfortable, dirty cars set aside for Negroes and then lecture all evening. Always there was the problem of where he could eat, where he could sleep. There were times when he had to tramp around for hours before he could find a place to lay his head.

"Is it worth it?" he would ask himself when he would see a sign that read: "Nigger don't let the sun set on you in this town."

"Is it worth it?" he would ask when on a broiling day he would have to climb down into the basement of a building to drink at a fountain marked "For Colored."

"Is it worth it?" he would ask when he had to mount long flights of stairs to a top floor lecture room or go up in the freight elevator.

For the sake of good will he bore all the indignities. For the sake of what he had to say he traveled and traveled. Nearly always he talked about the same thing—"The Life Savers of the South"—the sweet potato and the peanut.

And crowds came out to hear him. Gone were the days when he talked to a little group of Negro farmers sitting on the floor of a cabin. The halls he spoke in were seldom big enough to hold all who wanted to come. Sometimes more people were left outside than could get in. Sometimes when he spoke, the streets leading to the lecture hall were blocked. When he made a nine-day speaking tour in Texas, the State Legislature adjourned to hear him.

After a trip George Carver was always grateful to get back to Tuskegee. It took him a little while to bury the hurts. Then he would be at peace again, thinking it had all been for a purpose.

But even at Tuskegee his time was not his own. For one thing, there was his mail. It grew and grew until he averaged 150 letters a day.

Mail came to him from every continent in the world. "Advise us about our cotton." "Tell us how to improve our diet by using peanuts." "Help us with our agricultural program."

American farmers wrote to him. "A fungus is killing my peanut crop." "My sweet potatoes are not doing well."

American manufacturers wrote to him. "How can we dye our cement?" "How shall we go about turning peanuts into linoleum?"

He answered everybody—and he returned every check. He was still getting $1,500 a year, the same salary he started with. He didn't want more—his reward was in the things he was doing.

One man, Tom Huston of Columbus, Georgia,

wanted to show his appreciation some way. He had sent one of his chemists to Carver with a problem—the oil was settling out of his peanut butter—and Professor Carver had solved the difficulty. Huston kept bringing Carver expensive gifts, but the professor simply put them away.

Once Huston said to him, "Tell me, what do you want most?"

"I want a diamond," Carver answered.

Huston was terribly surprised. What would a shabby looking man like the professor want with a diamond? But he did as he was asked. He bought a fine diamond, had it put on a platinum ring, and sent the ring to Carver.

On the next occasion when Huston's chemist was going to Tuskegee to consult, Huston said to him, "Find out how Dr. Carver liked my present."

Dr. Carver was not wearing the ring. "Where's your diamond?" the chemist asked him.

The Professor opened the case that held his mineral specimens. There among the lumps of copper and quartz and mica which he had picked up on his rambles was the diamond.

George Carver wanted nothing for himself, not even the honors that came to him. In 1916 the scientists of Great Britain elected him a Fellow of the

Royal Society of Arts. In 1923 he received the Spingarn Medal for his work in agricultural chemistry. He prized these honors not for himself but for his people.

Newspapers and magazines wrote about him now. They called him the "Wizard of Tuskegee," a "Columbus of the Soil," a "black worker with white magic." He didn't want the publicity for himself. But he did want the world to know that a Negro could do whatever a white man could.

Always from his laboratory he came out with something new. Now it was a paint, or a dye, or synthetic rubber. Now it was a veneer made out of palmetto, wallboard made of cotton, paving blocks made of asphalt and cotton. Before he finished with the sweet potato, he had made 118 different things out of it. Before he finished with the peanut, he had made 300.

Sweet potatoes and peanuts. The South had really taken his life-savers to its heart. Sixty-two million bushels of sweet potatoes were being grown! Five million acres of peanuts were being planted!

Carver remembered the unbroken fields of cotton he had seen out of the train window on his way down to Tuskegee from Iowa. Peanuts weren't even a crop then. Now the peanut industry was worth 200 million dollars. Peanuts had become big business. Peanuts were the South's second cash crop after cotton. In Alabama the Governor had proclaimed a peanut week, and for three days a festival was held with floats and bands and a grand procession. A corps of motorcycle police had escorted Carver to the parade.

Yes, his ideas were taking hold. And now here were these young chemists who were picking up where he had left off. What he had done with the soybean in God's Little Workshop had not been lost.

Carver had been the first man in America to plant the Chinese soja pea, or soybean as it came to be called. He had been the first to take it into the laboratory and turn it into new products. Before he had worked on the peanut he had made soybean flour and meal and coffee, breakfast food, oil, milk. He had lectured about them. But he had not dared suggest the soybean as a crop to Negro farmers. It was too strange a plant. His people wouldn't know how to deal with it, he had thought.

Now other chemists had picked up the soybean. They had found soybeans could be made into plastic so strong that it could be used in place of steel. That was something Carver had never done—he didn't have the equipment for it.

Plastics that could be used instead of metals opened up a wonderful prospect. America had for years been worrying about using up her mineral resources. For once you have taken copper or iron or any mineral out of the earth, it is out and there is that much less of it. But plastics could go on forever. The supply of plants was not limited—you could always grow more.

At last businessmen were catching on to what he had been telling them for years. They were beginning to see what farms could do for industry. Henry Ford's research chemists were looking forward to the time when five pounds of soybeans would take the place of twenty-five pounds of steel in an automobile!

Professor Carver was modest about having opened wide the door to the synthetic kingdom, but chemists knew very well who it was that had started them exploring in it. In 1935 a group of scientists, together with farm leaders and industrialists, let Carver know they were planning a meeting in Dearborn, Michigan. They were going to usher in the "Chemical Revolution," and they wanted him to come and talk to them. They intended to discuss making things out of farm products—chemurgy they called it. They said he was the greatest chemurgist in the country.

At the time Carver could not go, but two years later when the invitation came again, the professor accepted. It was then that he met the man who was making his dreams come true.

If anyone had told George Carver that he would find himself comfortably hobnobbing with one of the richest men in America, he would not have believed it. If anyone had told Henry Ford that he would find himself absolutely at one with a Negro working for $29 a week, he would not have believed it.

But that's the way it was. From the first instant the two men met, they felt they would see eye to eye, and they did. Henry Ford was devoted to the soybean. George Carver was devoted to the peanut. That was the only difference.

To Ford, Carver was the greatest living scientist. To Carver, Ford was a man who had the same dreams as himself—and the money to make them come true. They went away from that meeting with plans to see each other at least once a year. They kept a conversation going from year's end to year's end.

Of all the products Carver himself had made, few had actually been taken up by businessmen. It gave the professor a lift to think there was at least one businessman who was using farm products in industry in a big, imaginative way. It gave him hope that the South of farms and factories he dreamed of would one day be a reality. He would not live to see that day, but he had done what he could to make it come. And as long as he lived he would do more.

Did One Man Do All This?

22

AT TUSKEGEE PEOPLE HAD LONG FELT PROFESSOR CARVER had done quite enough already. It seemed wrong for a man as old as he was to keep on slaving away in the laboratory alone. Besides, there was the future to think of. Who would carry on after the professor was gone?

"You must have an assistant," the president said.

"No, no! I have worked so long by myself I wouldn't know what to do with an assistant. He would just get in my way," Professor Carver protested. "If I don't do a thing with my own hands, I don't feel I know it."

"But think of the future! Who is going to continue your work at Tuskegee?"

It was no use resisting—the president was determined. One assistant was tried, then another and another, a whole succession of assistants. None of them worked out. Some found Dr. Carver so set in his ways that he was hard to get along with. Some couldn't understand what he was trying to do. So many came and went that Professor Carver finally stopped paying any attention to them.

Then one day in the fall of 1935 there arrived at the laboratory a young man who had recently graduated from Cornell University.

"How long will this one last?" Carver thought to himself as he shook hands with Austin W. Curtis, Jr. Aloud he said, "Look around, get adjusted. Over there is a room you can work in."

Then he went back to what he was doing.

The young man was not put out by being dismissed like this. He did exactly as he was told—he looked around. But he didn't look around idly. Among other things he saw some magnolia seeds. He knew they contained oil. Could not that oil take the place of palm oil in soaps? He began taking the seeds apart and putting them together again just the way Professor Carver had done with the peanut.

Carver went on doing his work, and Austin Curtis went on doing his. Day after day it was the same. The young man knew enough not to ask any questions unless he was stuck. Once in a while he reported how he was getting along.

"That boy has independent ideas," Professor Carver thought to himself. He liked that. It was good having someone working nearby who knew what he wanted to do and went ahead and did it.

From magnolia seeds the young assistant went to pumpkins. He wanted to try making synthetic leather out of them, maybe get some colors, too.

Dr. Carver watched the way Curtis tackled the problem. It was just the way the professor would have done it himself!

"He's one of my own sort," he thought.

The scientist was definitely warming up to his assistant. What else did Curtis have in mind? Carver wanted to know. He was finding himself captivated by this new young life that had come into his own. The young man was so able, so earnest, yet so simple and easy to be with!

"The old man has a son at last," people said when they saw the two together.

And it was true. Professor Carver had begun to feel towards the young man exactly as a father towards a son. Everywhere he went, his "dear boy" went with him.

"He will take my place one day," Carver said proudly.

On his side, Austin Curtis tried to do everything he could to make life easier for the old professor. Curtis saw to Carver's comfort, made him take care of himself, kept people from bothering him, talked for him. If Carver acted like a father, Curtis acted like a son, and both were happy. Certainly the professor had never been so happy at Tuskegee before.

He was getting on in years now. In 1936-7 he was rounding out forty years of service. How could Tuskegee show its appreciation for the man who had brought such honor to his people? Single-handed he had changed the pattern of agriculture in the South. Alone he had done more than any other force to bring about good will between the races.

It was decided to dedicate the whole year to honoring George Washington Carver.

Throughout that fortieth year people kept sending

in contributions for a bronze bust of the professor. Not that he wanted one. He wasn't asked. If it had been up to him, he would have gone off to the woods on the day it was unveiled. But Austin Curtis saw to it that he was there, and dressed in his best. His best, to be sure, was the same suit in which he had graduated from Iowa. People didn't know that the suit had a special meaning for Carver, that his classmates had generously bought it for him in those days when he had almost nothing to wear.

For the day of the unveiling, Austin Curtis had had an inspiration. Hundreds of guests were going to be present who had never seen Dr. Carver's exhibit of fibers, paints, stains, and peanut and sweet potato products. Curtis got the exhibit together and set it up in a room of the new library. To the exhibit he added the stuffed fowl from Dr. Carver's office and his geological collection. It all made a fine show, and Curtis took up a stand nearby to explain everything and answer questions.

Some of the trustees saw then for the first time what Dr. Carver's life work had been. They were all very much impressed.

"This exhibit ought to stay up all the time," they said. "Our laundry building is too small for the Institute now. It would make a very nice museum with this exhibit in it."

So everything was moved over.

A whole lot of other things went in, too. There was the skeleton of Betsy, one of the yoke of faithful oxen that had plowed the first fields of the Experiment Station. There were tall jars holding some of the huge vegetables that had been grown on the trash heaps. There was the beautiful blue powder the paint company from the North had wanted Carver to help them put on the market.

Dyes and paints, wall paper designs and wall board; mats and rugs; vases made out of Alabama clays; ornaments made of feathers and beads and mica; seventy-five pecan products; the 118 sweet potato products; many of the peanut products—all these went into the museum, and much else besides. Space was found for hundreds of Carver's lace designs and thirty-six of his paintings.

Had one man done all this? It seemed unbelievable. And yet how much more George Carver had accomplished that never could be put in a museum!

Many people in America had long wanted to honor the great scientist whose life had been one continuous giving. There was a clear and simple way to do it, and in 1939 they took that way. In the home of Theodore Roosevelt in New York City, before a group of 200 dinner guests, the Roosevelt Medal for distinguished service in the field of science was bestowed on George Washington Carver.

After that, honor followed honor, award followed award, till nearly every man, woman, and child in America got to know his name. Never had a man started so low and climbed so high.

The old professor accepted his tributes graciously. Then he went back to his work. Almost until the end came in 1943 his wonderful hands kept making things.

There were only two of the honors that he let his mind dwell on.

The first was that eighteen schools had been named after him. A school was a very precious thing to George Carver.

The second was a road marker put up by the Missouri Highway Commission to direct travelers. The sign read: "Birthplace of George Washington Carver, Famous Negro Scientist."

Back home in Diamond the white boys and girls he had played with as a child were now very old men and women. Carver liked to think they knew about the marker. He liked to think they were proud of their George.

Index

John Askling, indexer